"LiftOff Leadership makes a very real and useful contribution to the leadership library. Betty Shotton urges leaders to be in awe of many things including our lives, our surroundings, and the endless possibilities, but most important, to be in awe of leading. She teaches us to perform this noble calling with all we have, both mind and heart."

—Robert H. Moran, COO/EVP,
Aircraft Owners and Pilots Association

"Some people are born leaders, but many of us are brought into leadership positions with no clear road maps or checklists. As a woman who has been put into a leadership position often, I've had to evaluate what leadership means. Betty's book gave me insight and a valuable resource on what leadership means to me now, and how I can better understand my role."

—Patty Wagstaff, U.S. National Aerobatic Champion;
Inductee, National Aviation Hall of Fame

"In my own career, I have seen how the right guiding principles and values can unleash the full range of human potential. *LiftOff Leadership's* 10 Principles for Exceptional Leadership provide the checklist that leaders everywhere can refer to often in order to maintain proper leadership 'course and speed,' unlocking your company's engagement and innovation along the way! The book is as inspiring as it is pragmatic and a joy to read."

—Les Schmidt, CEO, Songbird; Former Chairman,
Golden Gate University

"LiftOff Leadership is a new and different approach to a topic that has been written about by numerous authors. For those starting in leadership as well as those who are established leaders, this book should be on the shelf in the office behind them as a guide that is easily accessible."

—Park Brady, Principal Executive Officer/COO of The St. Joe Company;
Former CEO, ResortQuest International; Air Force Fighter Pilot (ret)

"Betty Shotton shows us what a consummate executive should value most, both at work and in life."

—Harriet Levine, President,
Stuart Levine & Associates LLC

"It is fitting, given her aeronautical background, that Betty Shotton would provide us with a 'leadership checklist,' but what is notable is her ability to take the lessons of flying into other realms of business and personal leadership. This book is an excellent guide for those who seek to be pilots in their own right, whatever the field of endeavor."

—Paul F. Levy, former CEO,
Beth Israel Deaconess Medical Center, Boston, MA

"You will appreciate Betty Shotton's vastly different and much-needed approach to leadership. Test your own values with helpful checklists and operationalize 10 principles to soar into a better future with this book by a leader tested as a pilot, CEO, and consultant."

—Hon. Linda Tarr-Whelan,
Author of *Women Lead the Way:
Your Guide to Stepping Up to Leadership and Changing the World*

"*LiftOff Leadership* offers a unique perspective comparing the skills of government or corporate leadership with the similar traits involved in the operation of an aircraft. Success most certainly depends on the ten elements mentioned in this book. A breakdown in even one of these fundamental principles could easily cause leadership failure in business or unsafe flight operations."

—David B. Lehr, American Airlines/TWA Captain (ret); Florida Institute of Technology College of Aeronautics, Professor and Flight Operations Director

"Betty Shotton has captured the full essence of leadership by demonstrating the synergistic power of character and competence in *LiftOff Leadership*."

—Dr. Len Marrella, Author of *In Search of Ethics*
and President of The Center for Leadership Ethics

"The book clearly illustrates how principled leadership can co-exist in a performance-driven world focused on the bottom line. Understanding Betty's valued principles of leadership helps you and your team to meet or exceed its overall corporate goals while maintaining ethics and standards. Betty's book is a great read and a must for anyone who is a leader or aspires to be in a position of leadership!"

—Richard J. Walls, P.E., Director, NCDOT Division of Aviation

LIFTOFF
LEADERSHIP

LIFTOFF
LEADERSHIP

10 PRINCIPLES FOR EXCEPTIONAL LEADERSHIP

BETTY SHOTTON

BEAUFORT BOOKS | NEW YORK

Library of Congress Cataloging-in-Publication Data

Shotton, Betty.
LiftOff leadership : 10 principles for exceptional leadership / by Betty Shotton. -- 1st ed.
p. cm.
Includes bibliographical references.
ISBN 978-0-8253-0647-1 (hardcover : alk. paper)
1. Leadership. I. Title. II. Title: Lift off leadership.
HD57.7.S497 2011
658.4'092—dc23
2011020283

Published by Beaufort Books
www.beaufortbooks.com
27 West 20th Street, Suite 1102
New York, NY 10011
info@beaufortbooks.com

Distributed by Midpoint Trade Books
www.midpointtrade.com

Cover design by Sara Birkemeier, 8 Dot Graphics
Interior design by Maria E. Mendez, Neuwirth and Associates, Inc.

Printed in the United States of America

To those who are brave enough to follow,
may your leaders give you the wings you deserve to soar.

And to my husband,
Dr. Christopher J. Hyland

CONTENTS

FOREWORD

More than twenty years ago I started an airline with one plane, one route, and six employees. That airline, Cape Air, is now one thousand employees strong and lifts off from places as diverse as Cape Cod, Florida, the Caribbean, and Guam. So, the notion and metaphor of *Lift-Off Leadership* is close to my heart.

My journey has taken another dramatic turn, raising yet more questions about what meaningful leadership really means.

I now serve as a State Senator from Massachusetts, representing Cape Cod, Martha's Vineyard, and Nantucket. Leadership in the public and political world is very much on my mind as I represent a remarkable community, and engage in that process we all celebrate called democracy.

While Betty Shotton's fine book begins on a runway, in the cockpit of a Cessna, when we reach literary altitude it soon becomes apparent that leadership, well defined, is never a solo act. Any good pilot knows that he or she flies only because of a strong network of collaboration in every single aspect of the experience; from building the plane, to laying the runway, to creating airport facilities, to relying on air traffic controllers, an interwoven and remarkable infrastructure allows crisscrossing flights to move safely.

Only with all this in place do people soar.

So it is in every situation I've encountered.

The airline I'm proud to have founded now shares ownership with many of its employees because we all understand that it is collaboration that creates our success; everyone who has contributed deserves to be recognized and rewarded for that truth. And at the Massachusetts State House, as one of forty senators, I see how democracy is built on the same premise; true leadership must be defined by the strength of coalitions which result in compromises built on common ground, compromises that engage and bind while holding true to core principles.

And so leadership is not about pulling people from the front in a predetermined direction. It is about pulling people together to reach a shared destination.

Easier said than done. But three key tenets to good leadership that help to steady me, like three legs on a sturdy stool, are not abstract or complex:

Trust, which results in real collaboration.
Humility, which also invites inclusion.
Humor, which often helps carry the day.

Betty's exploration of leadership delves much more deeply into meaningful values and principles, helping us see how we can translate goals into strategies. Her insights and exercises combine; like a good flight plan, there is both a clear destination and plenty of detail for how to get there.

But unlike any plane ride, my sense is that the journey never really ends. Leadership always requires a form of exploration, both personal and social. We are asked to grow and explore new territory. That is leadership's beauty, and challenge.

So thank you, Betty, for asking me to write a foreword to your insightful book. I'm honored. More importantly, thank you for taking on such an important topic. What you've chosen to do, and how you've chosen to do it, is proof positive that *LiftOff Leadership* works.

Dan Wolf
Founder, Cape Air
Massachusetts State Senator
from the Cape and Islands

NOTES ON FLYING

When my flight instructor hopped out of the Cessna, said, "You're on your own, kid," and shut the door, I knew that it was my time of reckoning. As I taxied out to Runway 17 for my first solo flight, I struggled to master my emotions. I got into position for takeoff, pushed the throttle full forward, took my feet off the brakes, paid close attention to critical indicators and speeds, pulled back on the yoke, and up I went. Immediately the stark realization hit me: I was high above the ground and I was alone. There was no way down except through my own skill and resourcefulness. I understood for the first time what it really meant to hold my life in my hands. That solo flight drove home an extraordinary truth—no one can save you when you are alone and in command of an airplane. It is lonely at the top.

Everything else takes a backseat to this unique aspect of flying. Errors of judgment, poor decision making, imbalances, a lack of accountability, fear—any one of these can result in the loss of lives. Outside of a pilot's skill, integrity, judgment, and command, there is no safety net at 10,000 feet.

The same is true of leadership.

Leaders have as great an effect on the outcome of people's lives as a pilot in command of a plane filled with passengers. The impact of a leader's conduct and character is more subtle than that of a pilot's. But the consequences of their actions are every bit as pervasive and powerful in determining the trajectory and outcome of individuals' lives, and the likelihood that they will fulfill on their promise and potential.

Pilots and leaders. I have had the privilege to know many, and have personally experienced both roles. I am acutely aware of a pilot's responsibility for the safe passage of those on board and the equally critical responsibility a leader has to mindfully direct the lives of those under his influence.

The quality of our future rests largely in the hands of our leaders. It is up to our leaders to ensure that we stay aloft, that we don't come crashing down, and that we land safely at our destination. As you read this book, put yourself in the captain's chair; be the pilot in command. Gain insight into the impact your actions have on those who look up to you. Do you have the right fuel? Is everyone on board? Have you reviewed the checklist? Are you on the right flight plan? Are you on course for your destination? Will you make sure that we land safely?

Just as you want to believe that the person in the cockpit on your next flight will get you safely to your destination, so too is the wish for those under the influence of your leadership.

Yes, pilots and leaders have a lot in common. So strap yourself in and take command. Look out over the horizon and gain insights from an elevated perspective. Fly high, but always return to solid ground. There's a lot riding on you.

Betty Shotton
September, 2011

PREFLIGHT

We still have the possibility of building a civilization based on Man, where the importance of an enterprise is judged less by its financial profits than by the kind of community it creates; where the measure of a man is his own character, not his power or his wealth. If we have sufficient desire, we can still build a civilization whose leadership rests on the respect and confidence it instills in others and whose standard of life is the quality of life itself.

—CHARLES A. LINDBERGH (1902–1974)
(*Of Flight and Life*, Yale University Press: 1947)

It is an honor to be a leader. It is also a big responsibility. There are few positions that have such a significant impact on people's lives. Think back on your own career and recall the positive effects of a great boss or the damage wrought by a terrible one—being a leader can have powerful consequences.

This book is not about other leaders or bosses; it is about *you*. It is written to give you an opportunity to sit back and reflect on your own leadership character and conduct. There are many kinds of leaders, some exceptional, some mediocre, and some downright harmful. What kind are you? What kind do you want to be? What do you stand for? What effect does your conduct and character have on those you lead?

Wherever you are on the leadership spectrum, you can learn, you can change, and you can grow.

The starting point is knowing what really counts. This book is that starting point for you. It is an opportunity to examine what is truly meaningful to you, and to see how those things are reflected in your leadership. It is an invitation to step back and take a look at your leadership and its consequences. It is written with the hope than when you finish, you are clear about what you stand for and value the most. It is written in hopes that when you are through you realize that when all is said and done, how much you cared was more valuable than how much you earned.

Theory, scorecards, and financial acumen alone are not enough to make for a great leader. You also need strength of character to tackle big issues, face failure, resolve stubborn problems, and elevate perspectives. To be a great leader takes more than knowledge and expertise; it takes courage and integrity. To lead others through uncertainty and confusion takes vision and resolve. When the future is clouded by doubt, others must be buoyed by your commitment to what is possible and your unfailing faith in them. The strength of your character forms the foundation of your leadership. What is it made of?

Your character is made up of what you value, your guiding principles. Your character is defined by what you hold to be uniquely important and meaningful, both in life and in leadership.

What is it about you that inspires people and motivates them to work hard, with passion and with purpose? What do others see when you stand up and lead? Who do you choose to be?

- As a leader you can be profitable and provide meaning to those who do the work.
- As a leader you can choose to be accountable and require others to be the same.
- As a leader you can elevate perspectives.
- As a leader you can create a work environment that fosters cooperation, collaboration, and innovation.
- As a leader you can inspire others to reach for their potential.
- As a leader you can create a culture that delivers excellent customer service at every level, service that puts smiles on faces and makes people feel valued.

- As a leader you can make a day, a life, an organization, a community better because of your leadership.
- As a leader you can be trusted and respected.

OR NOT

You have choices. It's easy to get swept up in the distractions and forces of technology, always tethered, your intellect constantly bombarded. You can become so narrowly focused on numerical measures and financial reports that you forget the big picture. You can lose your enthusiasm and inspiration under the stress of long days and never-ending details. You can forget how much influence your leadership exerts on others. You can fail to recognize opportunities to bring meaning and purpose into the lives of others through your choices. You can resign yourself to cynicism and just getting by, rationalizing that the paycheck and benefits are more important than the quality of life.

OR NOT

To put the value of your leadership into perspective, think about some of the leadership disasters of the past few years: Enron, WorldCom, Lehman, BP, AIG, Washington Mutual, Countrywide . . . the list goes on. These are big names, but the same things happen on a smaller scale. Day in and day out, employees are negatively affected by the conduct of poor leaders, in retail stores, car dealerships, and restaurants, in sports, in politics, in churches and synagogues, in hospitals and nonprofit concerns. Whether you lead two people or head up a global financial institution with a staff of thousands, who you choose to be, the values you represent, and the culture you create have a decided and powerful impact on others.

It's a choice.

As a leader you can choose to *do good* and *be good*. Or not.

Over the past three decades, there has been a subtle but significant shift in the way we define leadership success and how we measure leadership performance. The value of a leader as a person who can move mountains and inspire others to achievement has been overshadowed by a focus on bottom-line profits. An emphasis on numbers has overtaken the requirement that leaders actually lead people and organizations with purpose and meaning.

The verdict is in. The past decade has shown us a financially driven path that discounts the relevancy of humanity is a path that can lead to disaster.

That is where we are today.

Not only has this financially driven leadership model that excludes humanity caused financial, political, and environmental damage, it has resulted in an erosion of public trust in leadership. What has traditionally been an esteemed and respected role is now viewed with skepticism and distrust by an overwhelming majority of Americans. According to the 2010 National Study of Confidence in Leadership by the Harvard Kennedy School Center for Public Leadership, 68 percent of Americans agree or strongly agree that we have a crisis in leadership today, defined as a lack of public trust and confidence in leaders in all sectors.

There is not much a leader can do if he does not have the trust of those he leads; a lack of trust paralyzes effectiveness.

As leaders, it is up to us to change this perception. We can do it by combining our business acumen and technical skills with principles and values that have historically been at the foundation of mankind's greatest endeavors and magnificent achievements. We can do it by balancing the financial and strategic demands of leadership with a recognition and respect for human dignity, and by consciously bringing meaning and purpose into our decision making. As Charles Lindbergh so succinctly put it, "If we have sufficient desire, we can still build a civilization whose leadership rests on the respect and confidence it instills in others and whose standard of life is the quality of life itself."

Practically speaking, as leaders we are neither well prepared nor experienced with an understanding and handling of the meaning of our work and our life. We are trained in how to make numbers work, how to strategize, how to direct, control, and produce results. But we don't spend much time considering the consequences of our actions and our character. We don't emphasize quality of life or measures of sustainability and stewardship in our strategies. It's time for us to recognize that we must lead with our hearts as well as our heads, to be exemplars of what is good and just in mankind.

It's time to chart a new course for leadership. Values need to be an integral part of business-school curriculum. Strategic planning should always begin with value clarification. Leadership development programs should include value clarification and associated training as part of the core curriculum. Human resource departments should incorporate values in job descriptions and in their recruiting. Most important, you can contribute to a new model of leadership by knowing what you value, the attributes that bring strength of character to your leadership.

The following chapters present ten leadership values—vision, altruism, courage, accountability, possibility, resolution, faith, integrity, balance, and awe—the finest and most powerful values I have witnessed in my thirty-five years as a leader and consultant. Altruism and integrity alone could have put a halt to reckless subprime lending. Accountability might have averted the fall of Lehman Brothers. All of these values carry a lot of weight and will keep you headed in the right direction, no matter what obstacles you face. In this book, I have defined each within the context of leadership, and examined them for relevance and consequences. I have peppered the chapters with true stories from my experiences as a leader and as a pilot. Each chapter ends with a practical, hands-on Leadership Checklist, which includes self-assessments and thought-provoking questions to further your thinking and increase your awareness of these values and the roles they play in your career. These checklists will help you gain unique insight into your leadership; there are no right or wrong answers, only room for improvement. It can be difficult to take a hard look at ourselves, but it is the first step toward personal and professional growth.

To follow you will find your own Preflight Checklist.

I encourage you to complete this before reading the chapters. (You can also download it on my website, at http://liftoffleadership.com/leader-resources/checklists-self-assessments.) While you are doing so, listen to your instinct and feelings. Listen to your inner voice. It holds the key to what you value. Then, as you read through the rest of the book and reflect on your personal experience and circumstance, what you know to be true and meaningful will surface.

Professional pilots refer to checklists before every flight. They know the consequences of missing something important in the conduct of their flight. I encourage you to do the same with your values. Check in with them on a regular basis. Your values can be your guiding light, your moral compass, but only if you are clear about what they are.

I hope that as leaders we are reverent in our responsibility to lead in ways that benefit those whom we lead. I hope that in our hearts we know what is right, and that we do the right thing. I hope that this book will elevate your perspective on the character of your own leadership. It is written for you, to strengthen your beliefs and provide practical guidance as you navigate the sometimes turbulent, always challenging, and constantly changing path of leadership. Our future holds more promise if we collectively as leaders insist that what we do is of true value and contributes to the world in positive ways. It starts with you and what you stand for and value.

So head on out to the launchpad and start the countdown. Enjoy the ride!

PREFLIGHT

The values and attributes that serve as foundations for your conduct and define your character are fundamental to successful and meaningful leadership. Below is a leadership value clarification exercise.

I. **Pick ten values that are most important to you as a leader.**

❑ Competence	❑ Kindness	❑ Faith
❑ Altruism	❑ Loyalty	❑ Focus
❑ Courage	❑ Optimism	❑ Honesty
❑ Assertiveness	❑ Decisiveness	❑ Patience
❑ Risk Taking	❑ Accountability	❑ Vision
❑ Possibility	❑ Balance	❑ Stability
❑ Authority	❑ Integrity	❑ Resolution
❑ Power	❑ Fairness	❑ Creativity
❑ Awe	❑ Fun	❑ Self-Confidence
❑ Independence	❑ Discipline	❑ Other: _____

II. **From the ten values you've chosen, select your five most important values. To help make this decision, take each of the ten and ask yourself how you would feel if you lost that value.**

MY TOP FIVE LEADERSHIP VALUES:

1. _____

2. _____

3. _____

4. _____

5. _____

III. **Answer the following questions to determine how well your values are represented in your leadership.**

1. Do you think the key people in your life are aware of your top values?

   Yes_____ No_____

   If not, share them and get feedback from them about how you exemplify these values.

2. Are these values evident in your leadership?

   Yes_____ No_____

3. What are the core values of your organization?

   1. _____

   2. _____

   3. _____

4. Are your own values in line with those of your organization?

   Yes_____ No_____

5. If not, how do you plan to reconcile this incongruity?

Your leadership conduct and character reflect your values. Be clear on what they are and consciously integrate them into your decision making and choices. Repeat this exercise annually, and refer to your core values on a regular basis. Lead within the broader context of what is truly meaningful and important to you. Let your values be your guide.

THE COUNTDOWN

10

VISION

I believe that this nation should commit itself to achieving the goal, before this decade is out, of landing a man on the moon and returning him safely to earth.

—John F. Kennedy (1917–1963), Speech to Congress, May 25, 1961

I was nine years old when Kennedy made this speech. I was ten when John Glenn became the first U.S. astronaut to go to outer space and return to talk about it. I clearly remember the day when all of us at Bedford Hills Elementary School were shepherded into classrooms to watch Glenn's space capsule fall out of the sky and splash down in the Atlantic Ocean. I was so excited, nervous, and curious about this amazing venture into space. I sat expectantly on the floor with a bunch of other youngsters, staring up at a grainy black-and-white TV. At first we could barely see the faint speck in the sky, and then we held our breath as *Friendship 7* appeared in full view and dropped into the ocean. It bobbed around, awaiting the arrival of a nearby destroyer, which came and hoisted it onto the deck.

Like a chick emerging from its shell, we watched in awe as the young astronaut popped out with a big grin on his face. It was a moment that united a nation.

Seven years later, Neil Armstrong became the first human being to step foot on the moon. These historical achievements were propelled by John F. Kennedy's extraordinary vision. With his promise of exploration into the vastness and promise of space, he galvanized the attention of a nation. He brought us together in a common dream. We were united, eager for accomplishment, proud of our pioneering spirit, a people joined together in the belief that we could do whatever we decided to do—even go to the moon.

How proud we were of our young astronauts! And how proud we were of ourselves! As a nation, as a people, we came together with the conviction that the sky was not the limit. We believed in our collective ingenuity, our technologies, and our leadership. During his short time as president, Kennedy helped us to conceive a dream for the future. He kept the vision before us as the resources were gathered and deployed, as interim goals were accomplished, step by step, until one day "we" did it. We landed and walked on the moon.

WHO CAN WE BE?

Who can I be? We all ask ourselves this question. It is at the core of our being. It is the root of our hopes and dreams.

Who can we be? This is the question that gives passion and purpose to organizations and teams. The answer provides hope and motivation when people come together for a common purpose. This is the question that drives vision and gives it power. It is a cry for meaning.

Visionary leaders are adept at providing answers to this fundamental question of identity. They are able to paint a picture of a desired future, and to capture the interest of others. They rally people behind a common purpose and propel them toward achievement by keeping the destination in sight. Once everyone is on board, strapped in and heading to the same place, visionary leaders provide the resources and plans needed to arrive safely.

VISION STATEMENTS

Examples of compelling and effective vision statements abound in business.

- NIKE: "To bring inspiration and innovation to every athlete in the world"

- HARLEY-DAVIDSON: "To provide extraordinary motorcycles and customer experiences"
- WALT DISNEY: "To make people happy"

These are clear examples of how a simple statement can mobilize and inspire a workforce. An authentic, shared vision statement can successfully launch new products and leave the competition in the dust. A great vision statement can reduce turnover and empower research-and-development teams to deliver world-class innovation.

Dr. Paul Farmer, founder of Partners in Health, envisions a world where humanity has broken free from the cycle of poverty and disease. His teams in Haiti have treated over 3.5 million patients. His work with HIV and TB has increased awareness worldwide. What started as a small clinic in a tiny village in rural Haiti has grown to an international organization that provides the structures and services to deliver on Farmer's vision. These diseases no longer have to be death sentences and can be successfully treated.

Shai Agassi, founder and CEO of A Better Place, envisions battery stations replacing gas stations on the world's highways. His work is paving the way for wide-scale use of electric cars.

Richard Branson of Virgin Galactic and Elon Musk of Space X envision alternatives for life beyond the limitations of earth, and are hard at work creating methods of space travel to take us into an expanded universe.

Amazing innovation arises when leaders can see beyond the horizon.

SHOW US THE WAY

Human beings yearn for leaders with vision. People have an innate desire to be a part of something greater than themselves, to make a difference and to leave a meaningful legacy for the next generation. People long for leaders who can bring out the best in them, who can help them realize and access their capacity to contribute, who can bring them together for a common purpose and a better future. They look for leaders who can paint a picture of a better tomorrow and follow through with the delivery of that promise.

A leader with a great vision can change the course of history. With visionary leadership, who knows what is possible? Peaceful coexistence between nations, opportunities in outer space, the salvaging of faith in our financial institutions, a world with clean water, clean air, and protected natural environments. If the right leaders with the right vision take the helm, we can be safe; we can be free.

Now more than ever, we as leaders need to be visionary. With an awareness of the scope and intensity of our future challenges, we must elevate our points of view. It can be difficult to see beyond our immediate predicaments and problems, but people will face the future with hope and positive expectation if they can see the light at the end of the tunnel.

AT THE HEART OF VISION

Foresight and an intuitive sense of what the future can look like come more easily to some than others. But whatever your level of mastery, we can all understand that the effectiveness and power of our vision is relative to our belief in it. If you want powerful and effective collaboration and a passionately driven group of followers, your vision must be authentic and heartfelt. All too often, vision is a superficially produced part of a strategic plan. When vision is manufactured or feels obligatory, it loses its effectiveness.

Vision is not a tool you can just pull off of the shelf and perfunctorily apply. It cannot be conveyed to your team through a hired consultant. You can't phone in a dream. Authentic vision occurs when leaders believe in a desired picture of the future, and share their energy and focus with their organization.

John F. Kennedy's vision to put a man on the moon was the real thing. He saw the power and potential that would be unleashed as Americans joined together and stepped up to the challenge to lead the space race. He didn't know how to put a man on the moon, but he believed it could be done. And NASA believed him. Its scientists and engineers were fueled by his belief. As a nation, we believed him too.

There is a story circulated among leadership consultants that exemplifies the pervasive power of Kennedy's shared vision. As the story goes, during the moon race of the 1960s, a journalist was visiting NASA at

Cape Canaveral (now called the Kennedy Space Center) when he came across three janitors cleaning a restroom. Being a friendly guy, he stopped and approached them.

"How's it going?" he asked.

In response, one janitor growled, "How do you think it is going? I'm stuck here cleaning toilets."

A little taken aback, the journalist asked another janitor the same question. He replied, "I'm feeding my family."

The third janitor was humming and smiling as he cleaned. "Why are you so happy?" the journalist asked.

The janitor replied with a grin, "Because I'm sending a man to the moon!"

As a leader, your vision must come shining through in your message. You can and should get input from staff members and others who have a vested interest in the future of the enterprise, but in the end, you are the one who will give the dream wings. And for this to happen, your vision must represent something true and meaningful for you.

TRUE INSPIRATION

After many years as a leadership consultant and CEO, I know that people are not motivated by their company's drive to make money. All too often I see stressed executives who think that their employees are somehow comforted by the recitation that they have to make cuts to make money. People understand the importance of profitability, of course, but numbers alone do not inspire them. They are inspired by the hope and promise of the grandest vision of who they can be, as individuals and as a team. Tell them what future they are working for and they will work their fingers to the bone to get there. They will even willingly make sacrifices. Tell them they are working for a number? Not happening.

Leading with a vision is exciting and inspiring. When I was the CEO of a vacation property business, I found that through a common sense of purpose and shared commitment, I was able to elevate staff perspectives above the incessant complaints and noisy nuisances of a demanding customer service business. With a shared vision, we were able to create a work environment defined by mutual respect and cooperation. My vision—*our* vision—was "the interception of entropy," a phrase from Max DePree's book *Leadership Is an Art,* which means catching things before they happen. And though some never really understood the true definition of the word "entropy," they understood that our vision created a work environment that was positive, proactive, fun, and rewarding, one that resulted in satisfied and appreciative customers. The interception of entropy took us out of the victim mode; we were no longer pincushions waiting for the next complaint. With *the interception of entropy* out front and center, we were constantly reminded of who we could be. We built a work environment that was positive, proactive, and really fun. Coming to work was generally something that we looked forward to.

Most important, we got ahead of the complaint curve. We instituted customer surveys and addressed the ideas and concerns offered as a result. We invited guests to join us in making their stay and their vacation home as comfortable as possible. We gave incentives to homeowners to keep their homes in tip-top shape and backed them with professional maintenance and housekeeping personnel. We did the work and we lived the vision. Just about everyone wanted to be a part of what we had: fun, respect, professionalism, and, not surprisingly, profit.

On the other hand, I have participated in consulting assignments where I was asked to facilitate the visioning process, with limited involvement from company leadership. In one instance, a CEO wanted me to work with the staff and let him know what they came up with. He attended a couple of the planning sessions and cheered employees on as they came up with a good vision and a supporting strategic plan. The staff worked hard, they collaborated, and they came up with a vision that they presented at a retreat, which the leader wasn't able to attend. The staff developed specific goals and strategies. They built in accountability and measurement. They did everything right. But just before they put the finishing touches on the documents, the leader called off the whole process. Something more pressing came up, and the vision receded from view. Resignation and a return to work as usual inevitably followed. An opportunity to elevate the morale and productivity of the group was lost.

Vision should precede tasks; otherwise you risk putting your staff on a hamster wheel: frantically running, trying to stay ahead of demands, but never getting to the desired destination. The visioning process can be laborious, and for a harried executive who just wants to get it done, it is easy to relegate it to the back burner time after time.

The irony is that once a shared vision is in place, tasks get easier because employees are motivated by a sense of contributing to something greater than themselves. It is worth the time and effort to get a vision in place, because with no compelling vision, work becomes little more than a series of distractions and detours.

In the case I just described, and in many others I have seen, the visioning process was merely the leader's idea of something that ought to be done. What was missing was an inspired, passionate, and committed visionary. Without that, the process loses its potency and allure.

Vision must start from the top, from the leader, the pilot, the person responsible for reaching higher altitudes and landing safely.

EXERCISING OUR VISION MUSCLES

Some leaders are born visionaries. For the rest of us, we need to strengthen the skill, like any muscle. Vision consists of a combination of skills. First and foremost is the creative ability to project into the future. Visionaries can look at whatever reality confronts them and intuitively see a way to successfully integrate today's realities with future opportunities.

Start with something as simple as your office space. Take a look around. Come up with a visual image of what you would like to see. Would you like it to be less cluttered? A different color, more room, something on the wall? Perhaps even a different office altogether? Create the vision, write it down, keep it in front of you, and start trying to create something different.

The process of writing this book was long and lonely, and demanded great attention to detail. It was easy for me to get bogged down and disillusioned in the task-orientation of book-writing demands. I needed to constantly elevate my perspective; I needed a compelling vision of the future. So I developed a vision of it as a real book, on a shelf alongside other leadership books at Barnes & Noble. I had a graphic designer sketch out a rough draft of the cover, and I hung that on my office wall in front of me. That vision sustained me through all the hard work and deadlines.

Perhaps these seem like small visions, but I offer them as examples of where you can start if your visioning muscles feel underused. When you have developed the skill, you can envision the boldest of plans, and then you can experience incredible accomplishments.

Visionary leaders are not just future dreamers. Their dreams are anchored by well-crafted, collaborative strategies and benchmarks, by discipline and dedication to the hard work and attention to detail that contribute to the dream's realization. Visionary leaders see the long term and have the ability to stand up against short-term expectations when they are not in the best interests of the organization. And visionary leaders are not top-down; they may be the primary movers of the vision, but they work together with those who will be part of its realization. A visionary leader brings others together in a common understanding of where they are going and what it will take to get there.

GETTING LOST IN THE TREES

There are many things that can impede a leader's ability to see the forest for the trees. Micromanaging others, being overly involved in the details, and poor delegation skills can all result in loss of vision by obscuring the big picture. Leaders frequently get trapped in a rat race of reports, meetings, and metrics, drowning under endless tasks and deadlines, all of which contribute to stress and burnout.

Many leaders lack confidence in others' ability to get things done. A complaint I often hear on consulting assignments is that leaders micromanage. They look over their workers' shoulders, second-guessing them, impeding their personal growth and development and stifling their creativity. As a leader, remember that micromanaging will only result in extra work for yourself and resignation and mediocrity from those you manage. People will lose interest in the big picture because they don't feel valued and their efforts are not acknowledged.

Instant gratification has become an entrenched characteristic of our society. We are bombarded by high-speed, instantaneous information from smartphones, laptops, iPads, and other technologies. We have become increasingly impatient and seduced into thinking we have to have *it*—money, success, the newest gadget, the girl, the car, the house—*right now*. Such thinking permeates our business lives, too, and translates into rapid, reactive decision making, focused only on the narrow opportunity at hand. A visionary leader needs wisdom and maturity to operate in today's world, and to maintain a big-picture perspective and a long-term orientation despite the "get it done *now*" pressure.

But no matter how strong a vision is, it will be ineffective if your commitment to it is superficial and perfunctory, as if visioning were itself a process and not a purpose. On the surface, a catchy slogan looks good, but watch out for words that are only words; without depth or meaning they will have no bearing on a long-term, sustainable vision.

Many institutions will proudly show you their vision statement. They will let you know that they paid a high-profile consulting firm a lot of money to help them arrive at this great idea. In many of these organizations, if you ask staff members what the company's vision is, they'll mutter something about having seen it somewhere but won't be able to call it to mind. But in an organization with a truly visionary leader, just about everyone can recount the company's vision.

RECREATING SISYPHUS

Organizations without a vision of the future often find themselves behind the curve of innovation, left behind as competitors seize opportunities and embrace new technologies, new discoveries, and new concepts. Visionless companies attract mediocre performance, staff members who show up just because of paychecks and do only what's necessary to get by, high absenteeism and turnover, and flavor-of-the-month projects. Without vision, jobs are just jobs, customers are easily lured elsewhere by a more energized sales offer, layoffs loom, and top talent jumps ship. When I see employees taking on one task after another with no clear idea of why their efforts matter, I am reminded of the Greek myth of Sisyphus, whose punishment was to push a big rock to the crest of a hill, only to have it roll back down, over and over again. Such is the subtle but constant level of frustration and despair that I encounter in many companies.

The true cost of not having a shared vision is high.

When you fly an airplane, your ability to know where you're heading, to understand your current position relative to the big picture, and to see and touch down safely on the runway are critical components to safe flight. For those who are not trained in instrument flying, the loss of vision or visual reference outside of the aircraft can be a matter of life or death.

Another obviously important aspect of flying is a safe landing. Pilots must be able to see the runway in order to land (though there are sophisticated planes with the capacity to land "blind"). If the weather is terrible and there is limited visibility, pilots use approach diagrams that specify the minimum safe descent altitude, and a certain height above the runway that when reached, if they can't see the runway, they can't land. Trained pilots never go below the minimum safe altitude unless they have the runway in sight. At the end of the well-laid-out path, a pilot needs vision to land safely at her destination.

In leadership, the runway is your goal; it is the place your vision has brought you to. Keep that runway in sight, as you constantly scan the activities of your organization, assessing the indicators of its health, making the small or large adjustments needed to stay on course. And all the while, just like a pilot, let others know where you are on the trajectory to the future, and let them know you are on target—500 feet, 100 feet . . . touchdown.

WHERE IS RUNWAY 5?

In the early-morning hours of Christmas Day, 2002, Runway 5 at Dare County Regional Airport in Manteo, North Carolina, was just out of sight for John Belnay. As he prepared for his return flight home, he knew that the weather at Dare County was below minimums for landing. But it was late and he had had a long day and wanted to get home, so he decided to try anyway. He had skirted in below minimums many times before. He knew the airport well and he was sure that he was safe from any ground obstructions on the approach to Runway 5, an old familiar friend, which came off of the water.

By most accounts John Belany was a loner. Thin and lanky, he wore a ducktail hairstyle straight out of *Grease*, a signature green army fatigue type of jacket, and always blue jeans. They say he was married once to a mechanic lady, with grease under her nails; didn't last long. What he was really married to was airplanes. No one was quite sure where he came from, New Jersey maybe, or perhaps closer by in rural North Carolina. He showed up in Manteo in the mid-1970s, and took on work as a flight instructor to adventurous locals, and occasionally flew charter flights for tourists.

Then one day, after twenty-five years of patching together flying work, he landed the coveted job of flying packages for United Parcel Service—a consistent job, a steady paycheck, and a turbine engine. The route he flew was routine and undemanding: Manteo to Edenton, to Raleigh, to Elizabeth City and home to Manteo. The biggest risks for a pilot flying that circuit were probably complacency and overconfidence.

I wonder if John felt a little bit like Santa when he loaded the cargo hold of his Cessna Caravan with packages on Christmas Eve 2002. With his sled packed and ready to go he took off from Dare County Regional Airport and headed first to Edenton. He didn't stay and chat, only lingered long enough to unload, and then off he went into the nighttime skies, headed to North Carolina's capital city, Raleigh.

John landed at Raleigh-Durham International around 8:30 P.M., unloaded, and hung around for a couple of hours. By 11:30 Christmas Eve he was fueled and lined up on the runway, and then he took off once more heading back east for one last stop to unload packages at Elizabeth City.

By the time he was ready to head home it was after 1:00 A.M. Christmas morning. The weather at his final destination, Manteo, had deteriorated well below the safe published minimums of 640 feet. He tried anyway, never making it safely home. A pilot can't land without seeing the runway, and that night the runway was completely obscured by a heavy fog.

As a pilot, I can tell you that there is nothing quite as welcoming as the sight of runway lights after flying in bad weather, relying solely on your instruments to guide you to your destination. Breaking out of the clouds and seeing that runway laid out in front of you is one of the most relieving sights I know.

A leader without a clear view of his destination is like a pilot flying around in the clouds—he may be getting close to the runway, but he won't be able to land until he can see it. As a leader, you need to be like a pilot: know where you're headed, provide a clear picture of your destination, make a plan to get there, and make sure everyone is on board. Stay on course, and when you have to deviate, make the necessary corrections. As you approach your final destination, let everyone know where they are; you are cleared to land . . . TOUCH-DOWN. Another successful landing. Vision accomplished!

VISION

The following questions and exercises are designed to support you in incorporating vision into your leadership.

I. Expanding Your View

The following exercise is for warming up your creative side. Let your imagination take over, have fun. Be a dreamer.

BECOMING A CRYSTAL BALL

Imagine your life twenty years from now. Write down possible answers to the following. The sky is the limit; just imagine and create what you'd like to see.

Will you be working?_____

If so, what will you be doing?_____

Where will you be living?_____

What kind of car will you have?_____

What will be the state of the world?_____

_____

What will be the newest technological advance?_____

What current technology will have become obsolete?_____

_____

What will be the primary source of fuel?_____

What new medical cures will be available?_____

_____

What has been the greatest discovery in your lifetime?_____

_____

What dream came true for you?_____

Now that you have widened your lens, move on to some practical applications of vision for leadership.

II. Vision in the Workplace

The following questions are for gaining insight into the use of an authentic vision in your organization.

1. Does your organization have a relevant and meaningful vision statement?

   Yes_____No_____

   If yes, write it here. _____

   _____

   If not, why not?_____

   _____

2. If yes, does the vision drive the company's strategic plan?

   Yes_____No_____

3. Is the vision integrated with operations?

   Yes_____No_____

4. Was the vision developed with input and communication from all levels of employees?

   Yes_____No_____

5. Does the vision have buy-in throughout the organization?

   Yes_____No_____

6. Is there a feeling of purpose and meaning in your workforce and in the culture of your organization?

Yes____No____

III. Taking a Stand for the Long Run

Sticking to a long-term vision can be challenging. Consider the following questions:

1. Would you be willing to risk your job, a promotion, or a raise by saying no to short-term growth and profitability at the expense of the long-term vision?

2. Would you be willing to show negative numbers in the short term in order to reach for sustainable future growth and profitability?

3. Would you be willing to say no to being evaluated solely on short-term expectations?

4. Do you regularly share your organization's vision with employees, customers, and shareholders, maintaining a long-term horizon for them in regard to the organization's direction?

IV. Practicing the Art of Visioning

There is a planning tool known as "future-scenario planning." It is used to encourage, support, and structure futuristic thinking in teams and organizations. It is best done with the guidance of a professional facilitator/consultant, but I will give you a brief introduction to it here. If you like the concept and want to implement it in your organization, seek a professional strategic-planning consultant to help you. There are several books on future-scenario planning as well.

A FUTURE SCENARIO

Start by imagining a possible scenario for your organization in the year 2025. Modify the template that follows so that it is relevant to your company. Then give the scenario to small teams (management and/or staff) and ask them to answer the questions that follow.

Your Future Scenario

The year is 2025. [Your organization] _____ is suffering a downturn and is in the third year of losses. After a long history of profitability and stability, competition from [another company] _____ is increasing, and two of your key team leaders are threatening to defect. [Your company's CEO] _____ is at his/her desk, located at [describe the building and location] _____, preparing for a three-day retreat for the executive team. The future is uncertain, and the pressure from all sides is weighing heavily on [the CEO's] _____ mind. Customers want concessions, employees want raises, the infrastructure needs attention, and every department has submitted a long list of necessary upgrades. The number one item on the agenda for the retreat is to discuss the vision statement that was made ten years ago.

Discussion Questions: In 2025 . . .

1. What is the size of the company?

   Employees _____

   Market share (%) _____

   Gross revenues _____

   Asset value _____

   Most profitable product/service _____

   Biggest line item loss _____

   Other _____

2. What are the company's primary products/services? _____

   _____

3. Where is the company located? _____

4. In how many different locations? _____

5. What are the key technologies that support the organization, and how are they falling behind the competition? _____

_____

_____

6. What is happening in the world that is affecting your organization?_____

_____

7. What are the greatest threats to the sustainability of the organization in the next decade? _____

_____

8. What are the greatest opportunities for the organization right now? _____

_____

9. What is the organization's greatest contribution to the industry?

_____

10. What is its greatest strength? _____

11. What is its greatest weakness? _____

12. Have each team present its future scenario at a meeting or retreat designed for that purpose. Teams can do it visually or orally. Use this technique in concert with your annual visioning/ strategic planning process.

Visionary leadership is a balancing act of creativity and foresight with strategic intent and delivery. Start with the vision and build the strategy around it. When people are brought together with a common purpose and a commitment to a shared vision, they can be unstoppable.

9

ALTRUISM

If there is one thing I've learned in my years on this planet, it's that the happiest and most fulfilled people I've known are those who devoted themselves to something bigger and more profound than merely their own self-interest.

—John Glenn (b. 1921), Astronaut and U.S. Senator

My father was part of a dying breed of physicians who regularly made house calls. He willingly left the comfort of his home and family after demanding twelve-hour days of patient care to attend to those who had no means to pay for or to be admitted to a hospital. He did it because he cared deeply for humanity. My father was a big proponent of altruism.

As a young girl, I loved going with him on these nighttime trips into neighborhoods that were as foreign to me as faraway countries. On one occasion I followed timidly behind him as he knocked on the front door of a dilapidated house in an equally destitute neighborhood. When the door opened and the awaiting occupants saw my father standing there, the look of worry and despair on their faces was replaced with grateful smiles and a sense of hope. I could feel their relief. It was like a breath of fresh air. We were warmly greeted and welcomed into their home. I experienced on an instinctual level what my father meant when he said it was better to give than to receive, that the gifts he received from the hearts of his patients were so much warmer and more substantial than tangible rewards. I felt it in my bones as a little girl in dark hallways where the sick were taken care of by a man who was there for them. My father was a happy and fulfilled man. His life was marked by caring for and giving to others.

Altruism means being there for others, moving beyond self-preoccupation, extending a helping hand, listening and giving generously without expectation of anything in return. It's the CFO who quietly cuts his own salary, without being asked, when layoffs are impending. It's the employee who goes beyond his job description to help an overburdened coworker finish a project. It's the leader who truly cares about life and livelihoods.

It's not always easy to not put yourself first. Most of us have dark sides to our nature; we are human. The fact is that altruism coexists with greed, dishonesty, and other examples of poor conduct. But in our humanness and as leaders, we always have the choice to either act on behalf of something or someone outside of ourselves or to protect our own self-interest. Altruism is always a choice. The decisions and actions of an altruistic leader arise from an awareness of what is in the best interest of the organization, its people, and its customers, despite the screaming ego that says, "Me, me, me!" When you capture the essence of altruism, you know that it is *not* just about you.

A TOUGH ROW TO HOE

Putting the interests of others before your own can be difficult to do. It requires a degree of self-sacrifice. Yet at our core, most of us want to contribute to others and to our world in meaningful ways. We know that self-indulgence is ultimately not satisfying. How do leaders get beyond the powerful lure of self-interest? How can you strike a balance between a healthy self-regard and conscious service to others?

Our culture has fostered an entitled, "What's in it for me?" way of thinking and sanctions behaviors that run counter to selfless giving. We are inundated with marketing messages that tell us that having more things is the only way to feel good, look good, and be liked. We are taught that in order to have a good life we have to be successful, "success" defined as money, position, and wealth. What is not emphasized is the value of a life filled with love, caring, appreciation, and respect, along with the rewards of a life lived in service to others, a life that brings meaning to the world.

Money by itself has no meaning. It is a commodity, merely paper and coins that are defined and regulated by institutions to serve as a controlled and orderly means of exchange. Money's meaning lies in what it can provide: at a basic level, food and shelter. The problem with money is that we forget that its meaning has to do with *quality* of life as opposed to *quantity*. Money and profits are a necessary and important component of our businesses, but always keep them in perspective. As a leader, remember to put profit into the larger context of the quality of life of those we lead and serve. When money and profits are the primary drivers at the expense of livelihoods, humanity suffers. Altruism reminds us to elevate the condition of our employees and make positive contributions to our communities— and make money at the same time. They are not mutually exclusive.

THE BOOMERANG EFFECT

When people feel valued and acknowledged, they are more productive and committed, which can translate into low turnover, increased sales, better accountability, and higher profits. Truly caring about your employees and customers will have positive effects on your bottom line.

Over the past few decades, the aviation industry has had its fair share of economic challenges and setbacks, but two airlines have consistently weathered the economic storms better than most: Southwest and JetBlue. One of the primary distinctions of these two companies has been the remarkable character of their founders. Both Herb Kelleher and David Neeleman have been described as leaders with a genuine desire to serve others. During their tenures as CEOs, both were respected and appreciated by employees and customers alike.

The continuing success of Southwest has been a testament to Kelleher's generosity of spirit. When all the major airlines were failing, crippled by overhead and ballooning fuel prices, Southwest continued to increase profits. When airline unions and management were enmeshed in infighting, the pilots of Southwest took pay cuts and continued to serve the flying public with courtesy and respect. Kelleher had the interests of others at heart, and in return he received loyalty and cooperation, assets that can't be represented on balance sheets but can make the difference between success and failure.

Neeleman also understood the power of altruism. In the face of stiff competition, he introduced JetBlue in 1998 as an airline that would "bring humanity back to air travel." Recognizing the nightmarish scenarios that travelers faced as airlines clamped down on costs, eliminated services, and alienated workers and pilots, Neeleman stepped forward with a commitment to give customers a positive flying experience. And it worked. When other start-up airlines fell by the wayside in the chaos of rising oil prices, JetBlue consistently maintained profitability and increased its positive reputation.

A July 2009 article in the *Harvard Business Review* suggests that altruism will be a necessary and important leadership attribute as we move further into the twenty-first century:

> Altruism is starting to be recognized as an important driver of the reputation and resultant loyalty of whole organizations. The leader who has an overarching awareness and responsiveness to the role that their organizations play as contributing something beyond the individual is becoming increasingly important in motivating and retaining today's employees . . . [in a time] when conventional rewards such as raises and bonuses are hard to come by.
>
> —Sylvia Hewlett,
> *"HBR Boost Performance by Tapping Employees' Altruism"*

THE POWER OF CARING

To understand the influence that you can have on the lives of others, think back to someone in your life or career whom you could depend on to be there for you no matter what—a parent, a friend, a spouse, a colleague. How incredibly meaningful was that person to you? *You* can be that person for as many people as you want; as a leader, your opportunities for altruism are exponentially greater than most. That is why an altruistic leader is such a gift; your altruism can make a big impact.

As a leader, something as simple as your demeanor can significantly affect others. Negativity and anger, or kindness and generosity of spirit, are equally powerful unspoken signals. Altruism in leadership starts with an awareness of the influence that you exert by simply being there. When a leader is in the presence of employees, her attitude, her demeanor, and her example are felt by everyone around. It is very important to be aware of and responsible for your attitude and your expressions. Anger, fear, selfishness, egotism, intolerance, judgment, righteousness, and negativity have a depressing and negative effect on those who are influenced by your leadership. On the flip side, joy, empathy, caring, compassion, hope, faith, love, inspiration, benevolence, optimism, and a genuine smile can make someone's day.

I had a consulting project in a large organization where the top executives each had administrative assistants. Executive offices were on the top floor, supported in the middle by legions of hardworking and very helpful assistants. I loved going to that floor because it was vibrant with the spirit and energy of the women (yes, all women) who served as conduits for the decisions and directives of the executives. It was a floor filled with laughter, playful banter, and productivity. That is, until the CEO arrived. Most mornings, he came to work as if he were carrying the weight of the world on his shoulders. He was stressed, impatient, tired, and worried— and everyone felt it. With his head down, he strode forcefully through the admin area, too busy to say good morning, too preoccupied to greet others with a smile. He had no interest in acknowledging this dynamic group of women who would bend over backward to get the job done.

People began to make up stories about why the CEO was so distant and cold. Many longtime, loyal, hardworking administrative employees took his demeanor personally. Others just decided that he was a jerk, and felt that if he didn't care, neither would they. All of this dissonance and resentment could have been vanquished with a smile, an acknowledgment, a polite moment of interested small talk. But this executive was egocentric and, despite coaching and counsel, never got beyond himself to contribute to the lives and careers of those he worked with in positive and meaningful ways. He demonstrated a lack of concern and awareness about the needs and potential of others. It was all about him.

Today, little remains of the once-positive and vibrant administrative floor; most of those employees are long gone, replaced by people who bow under the negative weight of the leadership, holding on to the job merely for the good benefits package and steady paycheck. Eventually the CEO was asked to leave the organization, but by then employee morale was at an all-time low. It would take years to nurture and elevate their trust and confidence, and bring back their productivity and commitment.

CHOICE CREATES THE FUTURE

During the recessionary years of 2008 and 2009, layoffs were rampant in the United States. According to David Goldman in a 2009 article in *CNN Money*, "The hemorrhaging of American jobs accelerated at a record pace at the end of 2008, bringing the year's total job losses to 2.6 million, the highest level in more than six decades. A sobering U.S. Labor Department jobs report showed the economy lost 524,000 jobs in December and 1.9 million in the year's final four months, after the credit crisis began in September."

In this environment, many CEOs slashed their employment rolls while continuing to increase their own compensation and award bonuses to other executives, despite huge losses on income statements and significant loss of net worth and profitability. At the same time, there were other, more altruistic leaders who reached out to their employees and empathized with their plight. They said, "How can I help make this work for the greater good of us all?"

BE A LEADER WHO REALLY CARES

It's a wonderful thing when leaders authentically care. With the responsibility for cutting the budget, Paul Levy, CEO of Beth Israel Deaconess Medical Center in Boston, took the high road. In the face of impending layoffs required by economic realities, he decided to take a walk throughout his hospital the evening before the dreaded announcement would be made. He engaged in conversations with the janitors, the technicians, the dietary aides. He reached out to feel the plight of the workers who were the heart and soul of the organization. The next morning, when he stood before a large company gathering, he called upon the employees' assistance. "I'd like to do what we can for the lower-wage earners. If we protect them, we have to make sacrifices" (quoted in the *Boston Globe*, Kevin Cullen, March 12, 2009). The room exploded with loud and enthusiastic applause. E-mails, phone calls, and personal offers flooded in, people expressing willingness to curtail their hours, give up some of their vacation time, and take pay cuts.

Another leader made a very different choice in the face of declining profits and financial setbacks. In 2007, Countrywide Mortgage CEO Angelo Mozilo took home $22.1 million in compensation and received an additional $121.5 million from selling off his shares of company stock. That same year, he laid off 11,000 staff members as his company's stock price plummeted 79 percent (Mozilo sold before the drop). As mortgage and real estate markets collapsed, due in part to irresponsible subprime lending practices under his watch, he walked away with hundreds of millions of dollars, leaving behind thousands without jobs, contending with foreclosures and splintered lives.

WHAT MATTERS THE MOST

Altruism is not always easy, but it is a choice, a choice that can elevate humanity beyond greed and selfishness. When employees have a sense of purpose, of belonging to something meaningful, they will make sacrifices for the good of the whole, will work long hours, and will be committed and caring. In business we sometimes forget this and slide into thinking that people are selfish and work primarily for money when, in reality, some of the greatest things ever created have involved little money and a lot of motivation and meaning. In the twenty-first century, the leader who is able to bring meaning to the mission of the organization and harness individual energy and commitment around that mission will be the success story.

Altruism can be as simple as a smile of encouragement, or caring enough to stop and listen, sharing the joys and pain of our common humanity. In what ways, big or small, can you make someone's day a little brighter or your organization's culture more positive? How can you improve and contribute to the lives of the people who work for you, or those who buy your products and services? Leaders can make money and be generous and caring at the same time; these are not mutually exclusive. When I am delivering a product or service that is of real value to humanity, people are more than willing to pay. You just have to put people in the business equation, not as a sideline. Everyone wants to be acknowledged and cared about. It is a powerful and persuasive motivator.

A BIG-HEARTED LION

When I moved to Duck, North Carolina, it didn't take long before I started to hear stories about Paul Shaver. He was well known in the emerging business community of the Outer Banks in the 1980s. He owned the only waterfront restaurant on the northern beaches. He also owned the most popular restaurant and bar down the beach in Nags Head. He and his partner built, developed, and owned Barrier Island Station, a large oceanfront condominium complex that at one point was the most popular timeshare resort in the country. Over the years, he created or partnered in at least six more start-ups that still stand as successful entities today. He was a wildly successful businessman.

It was hard not to know who Paul Shaver was.

To know Paul as an individual was as intriguing and impressive as his business ventures. Confident, cocky, and assertive, he was as much admired as he was respectfully feared. As a boss, he had a reputation for running a tight ship, holding people accountable, and demanding the best from his employees in the delivery of customer service. He had a commanding and booming voice and eyes that dug right into you; you couldn't escape and you couldn't pull anything over on him. But behind that powerful presence and strong will was a man with the heart of a lion. Although he had high expectations for his employees, he willingly gave back to them, and not just in the form of wages. He listened when they had problems, empathized with their challenges, and showed a genuine interest in and concern for their well-being. He gave his time, his interest, and, when needed, provided opportunities.

He loved his employees and was there for them. He didn't throw money at their problems; he gave them his attention, care, and guidance on how to help themselves . . . ultimately the better gift.

He truly cared for people, and they knew it. Despite the tough exterior and high expectations, he was respected and loved.

Not only was Paul Shaver recognized for his entrepreneurial success, leadership, and business acumen, he was also notorious for his love of adventure. The Paul Shaver I knew the best was Paul the pilot. He loved to fly. He started flying in his teens, had his license and bought an airplane by the time he was twenty-four. He flew biplanes, tail-draggers, helicopters, executive-styled twin-engines, and seaplanes. He was one of the first civilians to pilot a Russian MiG. If he saw something with wings, he jumped in. I knew Paul to be a courageous, fun-loving, and proficient pilot. What I didn't know was the extent to which he used his wings to help others. He had the means and was always ready to find a way to lift up people who needed it.

Paul died unexpectedly in an ATV accident on a mountain trail in the Appalachians, always the adventurer. It was after this that the many stories of his generosity and service to others started to surface. Posthumously, Paul received an honorary membership in the Shriners. Through the years he had dedicated countless flight hours to picking up and transporting burn victims to the Shriner burn unit in St. Louis, at no cost. And when Hurricane Katrina hit New Orleans, he got on the phone and coordinated and conducted relief flights of doctors and nurses, getting them into flooded hospitals and nursing homes, and bringing much-needed assistance to people who were helpless and stranded. And his generosity and selflessness extended beyond the sky: long before "battered women" was a recognized and supported cause, he personally funded a shelter and provided security to abused women in his community who had nowhere to go. He was as generous with money as he was with time and energy. He was one of the area's biggest philanthropists. His passion and love extended beyond what his money could buy, as is evidenced by his generosity and compassionate spirit.

His longtime partner Sarah said that Paul often expressed humble gratitude for all his good fortune and was dedicated to paying it forward. He could have easily just enjoyed the benefits of his hard-earned good life, but his heart called him to do otherwise. His rich life was made all the richer through his constant giving to others and willingness to extend a hand to those in need. The world lost a man with real character when Paul died, but he lives on in the form of the countless trusts and bequests he left, and in the heart and souls of the many people that he helped along the way.

What role can you play in improving the human condition? How can your community benefit from your generosity? What kind of difference can you make? You don't have to change the world (although you might), but you can make someone's career path a little clearer, create a fantastic work environment, help a friend through tough times. You can make a difference.

ALTRUISM

How wide is the wingspan of your contribution and caring for others? Consider these questions:

- Do you believe that the world will be a better place because of your leadership?

- Do you consciously strive to make the workplace a positive environment for all?

- Do those who work with and for you know you to be a person who cares about them and the organization?

If you answered "no" to any of the questions, start thinking of ways you can improve.

I.   Checking on Altruism
For the following statements, circle either (mostly) YES or (mostly) NO

1. I am kind and encouraging to employees.   YES   NO

2. I am approachable.   YES   NO

3. I am a good listener.   YES   NO

4. I have made a positive difference in someone's life/career.   YES   NO

5. I uphold ethical behavior in my organization.   YES   NO

6. The compensation structure of my company is fair, and not top-loaded.   YES   NO

7. When layoffs need to be made, I personally address those affected or ensure that they are treated with respect.   YES   NO

8. My employees know me to be fair and honest. YES NO

9. I give to nonprofit groups, relief agencies, and organizations that support those in need. YES NO

10. I have personally volunteered to participate in projects to help those in need. YES NO

11. My organization fosters a culture of giving and volunteering. YES NO

12. In performance reviews I am honest, direct, and compassionate while holding employees accountable to agreed-upon standards and results. YES NO

13. I am a familiar sight throughout my organization. YES NO

14. I am accessible and willing to listen to constructive grievances. YES NO

15. I encourage others to challenge me and to offer alternative solutions without fear of reprisal. YES NO

16. I would give up my position if it was in the best interest of the organization. YES NO

17. My organization has a good reputation in the community. YES NO

18. When the community has a need, we help. YES NO

19. I have a genuine interest in the quality of life of my employees. YES NO

20. My employees are proud to work for our organization. YES NO

21. My organization's service or product benefits mankind. YES NO

22. My organization has a thoughtful
    benefits package.   YES NO

23. I am nonjudgmental and respect diversity.   YES NO

24. I volunteer for kids/schools/community
    events/fundraising.   YES NO

My organization offers:

25. Ongoing development and career training   YES NO

26. Degree programs   YES NO

27. Childcare   YES NO

28. Flex time   YES NO

29. Coaching   YES NO

30. Recognition programs   YES NO

Add up the number of YES responses.

20 to 28 YES: Congratulations! Keep it up, and always look for more opportunities to demonstrate your altruism.

15 to 20 YES: Doing well, but look for more ways to expand your capacity to positively affect the lives of others.

10 to 15 YES: Need improvement. Go back through the list and identify some areas where you can improve and increase your contributions to others.

Less than 10 YES: Unacceptable. It's time to reevaluate your career and leadership and make a new commitment to altruism. The next exercise will give you some suggestions.

II. Putting the Gift of Giving Into Practice

Below is a list of altruistic activities to do in the workplace. Regardless of your score on the previous exercise, circle four that you will do in the next few months (though if you scored low, you could circle more than four). Beside each circled activity, write a date. Put these dates and actions on your calendar or to-do list, and stick to it.

1. Participate in orientation sessions for new hires.

2. Ensure that your organization has well-designed and well-attended leadership/management development programs.

3. Provide one-on-one executive coaching as part of leadership development.

4. Have a 360-degree review conducted on yourself, once a year, and communicate results and intentions to participants.

5. Conduct regular employee surveys. Communicate the results and address identified issues.

6. Conduct regular customer surveys. Communicate the results and address identified issues.

7. Set aside time once a month when any employee can come and talk with you.

8. Initiate a company-wide volunteer program to support community needs.

9. Establish a mentoring program for new hires and for those new to leadership.

10. Send personalized birthday cards to your employees.

11. Hold a hand of or put an arm around someone who needs encouragement.

12. Greet employees at the front door at the beginning of a workday.

13. Spend some time in a different department once a month.

14. Educate employees on the fundamentals of departmental/company budgets and teach them to understand the connection of their work to the financial success of the whole.

In the end, our lives and our leadership will best be remembered by how much we cared, not by how much money we made. What will your legacy be?

8

COURAGE

Courage is the price that life exacts for granting peace. The soul that knows it not, knows no release from little things; knows not the livid loneliness of fear, nor mountain heights where bitter joy can hear the sound of wings.

—AMELIA EARHART (1897–1937)

Courage enables you to take action in the face of overwhelming odds and frightening uncertainty. It is wisdom and experience combined with confidence in your ability to rise above adversity. Courage is a strength that allows leaders to try something different, to introduce new products, to strive for excellence. Courage propels leaders beyond disappointment, loss, and failure, continuing the quest for achievement and contribution. Courage gives leaders the strength to admit their mistakes, to be honest, and to respect their own and others' vulnerabilities and weaknesses along the path of growth and development. Courage enables leaders to put their egos aside and make decisions that serve the greater good, even at the risk of their careers, their salaries, and their own job security.

LIFTING THE VEIL OF FEAR

Courage starts with the humility to acknowledge your fears. It is fortified through taking action in the face of those fears. As you continue to take on more challenges, your capacity for courage expands. Courage is amplified by the strength of your commitment to get to the other side of your fear.

In September of 2005, the magazine *Fast Company* published a list called "The Courageous Few," recognizing ten leaders who exhibited outstanding courage in doing the right thing. On that list was Eileen Collins, the first female commander of a space shuttle—specifically, the first shuttle launch since the *Columbia* disintegrated on reentry. Also mentioned was Michael Cappelas, the former CEO of MCI. He had the strength of character to take on the old WorldCom, which had fallen into bankruptcy under the leadership of Bernie Ebbers and an $11 billion accounting fraud, and turn it into a viable company. Another person on the list, Sherron Watkins of Enron, had the courage to speak up against the deceptive and fraudulent accounting practices that would later implode the company, taking down jobs, investors, and customers.

I have worked with many leaders facing a diversity of challenges. Once I coached a director who was in charge of a department that had been through the wringer of a series of poorly executed organizational changes. The group was demoralized, insecure as a team, afraid for their jobs, and distrusting of anyone associated with management. Their new leader was known for his turnaround skills. He was a very logical, strategic, and results-oriented individual, and he was going to make sure that this department delivered. He was big on execution but short on empathy—and empathy was exactly what the team needed.

By the time I was called in to facilitate, both sides had put up walls and staked out their positions. The team had withdrawn from supporting their new leader, whom they perceived as cold and capable of another devastating reorganization. The director had thrown up his hands in despair, resentful of this uncooperative team that seemed more concerned with self-pity than productivity.

The answer to the hostile impasse came in a meeting where the director authentically expressed his frustrations and admitted to his lack of empathy and compassion—a courageous act for a man steeped in the management philosophy of never showing weakness to employees.

He asked for their help. They paid attention.

With further open discussion, an environment of trust was finally established. Today that department is a joy to behold. The director is on his way up, continuing to develop a strong leadership character as he faces difficulties, develops his skills, and overcomes his limitations. Courage works; it will push you forward, making you stronger from the experience and better prepared for the next challenge.

It can be tough to handle personal attacks and negative agendas while holding on to your courage and confidence. But courage in the face of doubt and derision is crucial, as the path of leadership is littered with obstacles. I have had to close down offices and shut down businesses. I have had to lay off employees and conduct hundreds of exit interviews. I have always done so with as much communication, empathy, and focus as possible. It took courage, but while building and running a company, avoiding taking on tough challenges often means running the risk of losing it for everyone. There are many occasions when you as a leader are asked to rise above your own limitations and lift the veil of fear from your and others' eyes as you face adversity together.

FINDING YOUR COURAGE

What is this inner strength that the lion in the *Wizard of Oz* so longed for? Where do you find it, how do you harness it, and how can you increase its intensity? Courage, like hope, faith, and love, resides in the inner depths of our human spirit. It has no physical qualities; it can't be detected through any of our normal five senses. Courage is internal, and its level unique to each individual.

I like to think of courage as a pilot light—a small flame that resides in your heart that is always there for you. The word itself actually comes from the French word for heart, "coeur." But why are some pilot lights difficult to engage while others ignite and grow stronger at the slightest touch? Why do some people have more courage than others, and how can you increase your own?

Cultural and social upbringing play a large role in the development of courage. If you were raised in a very protective and nurturing environment, you might not have had much occasion to call forth and exercise your courage. If when you fell off your bike, your mother picked you up and took you home, rather than encouraging you to get back on the bike and face your challenges, then you may have learned dependency and retraction. On the other hand, if your parents encouraged self-sufficiency and independence, you probably developed more strength and courage.

From an outsider's perspective, it is convenient to think that high-profile leaders were born confident, but when you take a closer look at the biographies of great people, more often than not they faced many challenges in their road to adulthood. It is not a coincidence that many of history's greatest leaders came from humble and difficult beginnings.

Sam Walton, the founder of Wal-Mart, was raised on a farm during the Depression. He moved many times as a child watching his father struggle to earn a living for his family. Sam grew up milking cows and delivering papers and doing whatever chores needed to be done to help the Walton family make ends meet.

Abraham Lincoln grew up in a log cabin, in rural Kentucky with only eighteen months of formal education. He taught himself. His parents were illiterate.

Colin Powell grew up in Harlem, the son of immigrant Jamaican parents.

Warren Bennis grew up in a hardworking, middle-class Jewish family in Westwood, New Jersey. It was his childhood challenges, his military experience, and his slow but steady climb up the academic ladder that allowed him to become one of the greatest experts and thinkers in leadership today. History proves time and time again that adversity and challenge are great opportunities for building courage.

In his book *Losing My Virginity* (Three Rivers Press 1999), Richard Branson, the wildly successful CEO of Virgin Group, relates a story from his childhood. His aunt bet him that he could learn to swim while on a family vacation at the shore, and he tried but was unsuccessful. On the way home, they were driving alongside a swiftly flowing river. Branson asked his mother to stop the car so that he could try once more to win that bet. She agreed and promised to pick him up upstream. In he went. The current was strong, and his family members watched as he struggled to stay afloat. In that moment, with no one jumping in to save him, facing the prospect of drowning, he figured out how to swim. This ability to take on a frightening and challenging situation has helped him become one of the most successful businessmen in the world.

Some leaders come into their positions with more courage than others. But the good news is that courage is an attribute that can be developed, strengthened, and fortified through practice. Courage-building starts with a commitment to recognizing, identifying, and stepping up to your fears. For some, that might mean something as simple as going to a movie or taking a trip alone. For others, it might mean addressing a contentious audience in the midst of an organizational controversy. No matter how strong your flame of courage, it will get brighter as you tackle your fears and challenges.

When I entered the MBA program at the College of William and Mary in 1978, I was oblivious to the scope of the challenges I would encounter. I was one of only two students in my class who did not have a financial undergraduate degree, and the first year was unbelievably difficult. Sitting in my first week of class in managerial economics, I realized that calculus (which I had never taken) was a foundation course. It was assumed that you knew it. I had to teach myself calculus while taking a full load of other subjects that were completely new to me. I wrote the ten derivatives on my hand before every class to help me. By the end of the first semester, I weighed only ninety-five pounds. I was paying my own way, working two part-time jobs at night, and receiving absolutely no help from my parents, who thought I was nuts to get an MBA when finding a rich husband was a lot easier.

What didn't kill me, however, certainly made me stronger—and more courageous. That first year at William and Mary was pivotal for the strengthening of my leadership character. The hardships I faced and the fears I overcame taught me that I was capable of just about anything I set my mind to. That year gave me a new sense of self-confidence and a much stronger flame of courage.

THE TOUGH-GUY FAÇADE

Bravado, or blindly walking into daunting challenges with no preparation whatsoever, is often mistaken for courage. Courage is not blind—behind it lies careful preparation, consideration, assessment, and planning. Courage radiates from well-earned self-confidence, not arrogance. Behind true courage lies humility, recognition of human frailty, and our individual efforts to rise above our own limitations with grace. You wouldn't attempt open-heart surgery without a medical degree, nor would you hurl yourself down an icy incline and attempt an Olympian ski jump without practice. But some leaders, buoyed by a reckless, often arrogant sense of machismo, will address long-seething, complicated issues with aggression and a misapplication of executive power. This type of bravado actually masks fear.

Other signals that are cover-ups for insecurities and fears are drinking, drugs, aggressive behavior, intimidation, bullying, and inappropriate relationships. Leaders have big shoes to fill and again are important role models. It is incumbent on them to overcome the haunting voices of the past and self-limitations that hold them back from true expression and meaningful leadership.

A FIVE-STEP COURAGE-BUILDING PLAN

It's always helpful to have a structure to keep you on track, especially when things are tough and unpredictable. As you face an uncertain and formidable difficulty, refer to the five courage-building steps below to fortify your courage:

1. Identify your fears.
2. Assess what you need and gather your resources.
3. Do a few dry runs.
4. Take action in the face of your fear.
5. Learn from your mistakes.

Now let's look at these steps in detail.

1. Identify your fears.

Sometimes it is hard to identify our fears because people are adept at suppressing them, especially leaders, as fear could be perceived as weakness. Often we cover up our fears with false bravado or downplay something's importance when in fact we are intimidated. The development of courage starts with a willingness to identify and admit your own unique fears. Everyone has them. Great leaders understand and grow from this.

Start by being honest with yourself. What makes your stomach tighten and your palms get sweaty? Here are some common fears that hinder leaders' ability to fully reach their potential:

- Fear of conflict. This can cause leaders to avoid controversial performance issues.
- Fear of failure. This makes some leaders dismissive of innovative and out-of-the box ideas.
- Fear of rejection. This can keep leaders from standing up for an unpopular person or principle.
- Fear of what others may think. This is a common deterrent to authentic and truthful leadership, and it can cause potentially important ideas to be lost.
- Fear of not being liked. This is a strong motivator for workaholics and leaders who sacrifice their relationships, their health, and their happiness in an obsessive drive to please others—at the expense of everyone involved.
- Fear of abandonment. This can lead to unhealthy and unresolved poor relationships.

These are just a few common fears. Everyone moves into adulthood with an array of fears generated by childhood experiences. It is part of your journey as a leader to identify your fears and take action to overcome those that impede your path to greatness.

Sadly, many organizations and countries are led by individuals with low self-esteem, an internal fear often masked by arrogance, authority, and intimidation. This is evident in the bullish behavior of politicians and dictators. It can be seen in the arrogance of financial CEOs who without their billions might be exposed as insecure and afraid.

Recently I was at a conference where I had planned to make a connection with a CEO who had international exposure and connections that would be beneficial to my business interests. I went to his organization's exhibit area and saw him talking with a group of people. As it happened, I had had a particularly frustrating and disappointing day, and my confidence was low. As I surveyed the scene and observed the CEO, my internal voice started telling me all the reasons that he would have no interest in me. But my commitment and conviction overcame my fear. My pilot light came on and I went up to the CEO and introduced myself, and we ended up having a meaningful and mutually productive conversation. Luckily, I was aware of my fear and knew how to quiet that childhood voice and take action despite its pleas to cower.

The more you practice and learn to face and overcome your fears, the more courageous and confident you will become. Eventually you will develop the heart of a champion and become a leader who instills confidence in others during the most formidable of challenges. And as you move up into even higher leadership altitudes, you will continually need to access, harness, and apply your courage to problems that once seemed insurmountable.

2. Assess what you need and gather your resources.

A very common fear is that of flying, especially in small, single-engine planes. Imagine that you confronted that fear by hopping into the pilot's seat of a Cessna 172, grabbing the checklist, following the instructions, and heading out to the runway for takeoff—without ever having taken a lesson. That would be reckless and dangerous. In overcoming fear—emotionally driven fear in particular—a lot of focus and attention are required to prepare for confident action.

Once you identify a barrier to progress that you are reluctant to face, investigate what learning tools are available to you. For executives entering into new arenas, like a new company or more responsibility, mentoring can be an invaluable asset. Someone who knows the ropes, who has been there before and can advise and counsel you, can be the difference between success and failure. If you are dealing with the fear of not being good enough, psychological counseling is worth trying. If you are afraid of failure and you are faced with the decision to take your company in a new and unfamiliar direction, executive coaching programs designed for executives at respected business schools, leadership development classes, and targeted readings are all good options. Whatever it is that stops you, seek out as much information about it as possible, gather your resources, and increase your understanding and knowledge. Courage is best accessed with an arsenal of knowledge and lots of preparation.

3. Do a few dry runs.

Continuing to increase your capacity for courage is like learning any new skill. As you move up, conquering one fear after another, you start small and then move into the big leagues as you practice and perfect. Ski jumpers don't start doing backward 360s on massive jumps; they start with little jumps and work their way up. If you are afraid of what other people think, start by going somewhere alone that makes you nervous—maybe a movie or a restaurant. If failure is an issue, learn a new and challenging sport where you have to be a beginner, or learn a foreign language in a classroom setting. If you put yourself in positions of not being competent, you will start to get comfortable with not knowing the answers and not being right. Conquer some dry runs before taking on the real thing.

4. Take action in the face of your fear.

With some dry runs under your belt and a strong knowledge base, you are ready to take action. Visualize a successful outcome. Get a good night's sleep and eat well. Do a quick assessment to make sure you have the necessary tools to support you as you courageously face something that you have been afraid of. Quiet your internal naysayer; brush the childhood demon off of your shoulder. Remember past accomplishments that you once thought daunting and impossible. Think of what others have done: Olympic athletes, soldiers in war-torn countries, people trying to recover after natural disasters. It helps to put things in perspective.

If it's a speaking engagement in front of a large audience, make sure you are relaxed, and have notes and audio/visual prepared and ready. If it is a performance review with a potentially hostile, aggressive, or defensive individual, make sure you engage in some kind of relaxation beforehand, and then review your notes and make sure you have supporting documents with you. If it is a contentious board meeting, get centered, be prepared, elevate your perspective above your own concerns, seek resolution and collaboration, and enter the meeting with confidence. Whatever it is that you must face, face it with the confidence that you are well equipped to handle the situation and the consequences.

5. Learn from your mistakes.

As you address your fears and face difficulties, you will have some successes and some failures. It's important to not beat yourself up when you don't succeed or do things perfectly. Instead, pat yourself on the back for trying, recognize your efforts, and have the insight and courage to look at where you were lacking or what you might have overlooked or missed. And try, try again.

Before I had my instrument rating, with no experience in the surreal world of flying in the clouds with no visual reference outside of the cockpit, I was intimidated by "flying blind." It was hard for me to feel confident when I first entered dark clouds and rain and felt the initial disorientation that affects pilots who are untrained and unskilled in the use of instruments. The only way to address that fear was to be trained by an instructor, to study, to learn about weather and the physics of instrument flight. And then I had to practice. Starting with little steps, I flew on cloudless days in smooth air with my flight instructor. We flew simple approaches. Then we progressed and tackled real weather issues: rain, fog, crosswinds, turbulence. He pushed me into bigger airports and more complicated approaches. It was like learning a foreign language. I did what I was supposed to do, but it was uncomfortable. I continued to make mistakes, and it was frustrating and exhausting. One day, in total frustration after botching an instrument landing system approach, we landed and shut down the engine. I jumped out, stomped my feet, and said "I quit"—which of course I didn't. And just a few days later, it all clicked: the scan became automatic, I learned to interpret the information and make the approaches accurately and successfully. At the same time, my nervousness was allayed and my confidence and courage soared.

That came in handy when I needed to land a plane in pounding rain, wind shear, and low visibilities. Added to those deteriorating conditions was a busy air traffic control with their hands full of planes trying to land at a field socked in by bad weather. As I got close to touchdown, they changed my instructions and sent me to a parallel runway. That last-minute switch meant having to change all the radio and navigational frequencies, pulling up a different approach plate, and adjusting to a totally different set of instructions. All my hours of training and the persistence of my instructors came into play then, allowing me to focus on the intended outcome and not be distracted by all the things that could go wrong.

People are affected by how you lead. Do you do it with courage and confidence or fear and intimidation? You have the opportunity to enhance and elevate the lives of others, to recognize and encourage their potential. You also have the opportunity to dictate, to squash innovation and enthusiasm, to incite mediocrity and cynicism. When your future is filled with challenge, uncertainty, and adversity, face it, figure it out, gather your resources, and do what it takes to move beyond difficulties and limitations. Your internal flame of courage will get stronger and light the way down the challenging paths you have to take.

CAN YOU SEE THE RUNWAY?

We rarely get to choose when courage will be required of us. It is the unexpected guest, the unanticipated call.

Courage dialed my number on October 3, 1996. A high-ranking official in the U. S. Surgeon General's office needed to get to the nation's capital. I scheduled the flight to DCA for the next evening. It was one of my first commercial flights, into one of the busiest airports in the world, in a single-engine Cessna 182, at night—all unchartered territory for me.

I knew that this flight would be challenging and filled with firsts, so I called all my flying buddies, hoping for a DCA-savvy flight companion to help me out with technical and moral support. No one was available. The realization that I would be on my own, flying a passenger into Washington, D.C., for the first time, was pretty frightening. So I did what I usually do when I am afraid: I prepared like crazy. I studied charts, approaches, and airport particulars. I made a detailed flight plan and an arrival reservation. I asked others who had done it to share their experience with me, and I got advice on what I could I expect.

October 4 dawned clear and blue, and was forecast to remain so through the evening. At 5:00 P.M., I headed to First Flight airstrip in Kill Devil Hills, North Carolina, to pick up my passenger.

Taxiing toward the tie-down area, you couldn't miss him; he was the only person in a tailored suit, with a hefty briefcase by his side. He requested to sit in the right seat with a headset, which only deepened my anxiety, knowing he would hear and see everything.

The flight up was uneventful, and by the time we were north of Richmond, Virginia, the night was pitch black. Close to the airport, ATC (air traffic control) authorized me to descend. The controller asked if I could see the runway. Well . . . Washington, D.C. at night looks like an extravagantly lit Christmas tree. Runway lights are kept low, and for a newcomer like me, they were indistinguishable from road lights, car lights, mall lights, and house lights. It was all a big merging maze of lights.

"Negative," I said.

The controller put me on a 360.

Coming around, he asked again if I could see the runway. I couldn't. Knowing that my passenger was listening turned up the stress level. With forced casualness, I asked him if he could see the airport. He said no.

"Negative," I said again to the controller. I sensed a bit of exasperation from him; this was, after all, the busiest airspace in the country, not a place for initiates.

Another 360. I strained to focus.

After the third 360, I remembered I could ask for vectors. I did, and to my relief, Runway 19 finally appeared in front of me. I landed the plane and we taxied to Signature Flight Center, a terminal for private and corporate planes. My passenger was polite but short on conversation. Once inside, he was whisked away by a waiting limo, while I took a few moments for some deep breaths and regained my confidence for the trip back.

Once again, I made all of the preflight preparations, got my clearance, and taxied out to Runway 19 for takeoff, homeward bound and alone. As I lifted off, the engine missed. Climbing out, it missed again, and again. I reported the engine roughness to ATC and requested a climb to 12,000 feet, where I hoped I could diagnose and correct the problem. I was reluctant to return to the same controller I'd just spent too many 360s with, feeling dumb. But courage can show us where pride sets us back. Twenty miles south of D.C., with no improvement, I decided to turn back. The risk of engine failure at night was too great.

The good news was that with my very recent experience, I now could easily identify the runway. I descended, landed, and humbly returned to the now-familiar private terminal. It was embarrassing to show up at the front desk of Signature again, but I had made my decision, and I swallowed my pride.

It took until the next morning to find a reciprocating engine mechanic in the turbine world of an international airport. The culprit turned out to be fouled spark plugs. Not a big thing on the ground, but a challenging uncertainty in the air.

With experience, I became proficient and comfortable in a Class B airport. I went on to fly my 182 into DCA, LaGuardia, and Newark many times. What had initially tested my courage became another skill I mastered.

When I go over in my mind the chain of events of that first foray into the congested airspace of Washington, D.C., I realize that though I was challenged, I stayed focused, made decisions, regrouped, and moved on. That was a difficult trip, but it was well worth the experience and the added courage that it gave me.

Constantly call on and increase your capacity for courage. It will strengthen your leadership. You are the one who has to make the tough decisions and take people into uncharted airspace. When you are placed in situations requiring courage, don't shrink away, rationalize avoidance, or blame others. Gather your resources and take action in the face of your fears. Your capacity for courage will increase, opening the way for ever-expanding opportunities and discoveries along your leadership development path.

COURAGE

To strengthen your courage, start with an honest assessment of the situations, relationships, and events in your life and leadership that you avoid or are hesitant to address.

I. **Identify a situation you are avoiding that seems risky or clouded by indecision and doubt. (Examples could be an antagonistic coworker, a rocky relationship, a career change, or an important strategic decision.)**

    _____

    _____

    A. List the reasons you are avoiding it.

        _____

        _____

    B. List three possible actions you could take to address the situation. Beside each, describe possible negative and positive consequences.

          ACTION   CONSEQUENCE

        1. _____   _____

        2. _____   _____

        3. _____   _____

C. Now take yourself out of the equation. Without thinking about your fears, circle the action that would serve the greater good of those involved in and affected by the probable outcomes. Pick the one that you know is the right choice.

D. In contemplating the above situation, what do you need to learn, what skills do you need to acquire, and what resources do you need to gain the confidence necessary to take the desired action ?

1. _____

2. _____

3. _____

II. **Be proactive, get prepared, gather your resources, and seek advice.**

III. **Commit to taking action by _____ (date).**

Return to this exercise as you continue to grow and confront fear after fear. It will help to strengthen your capacity for courageous decision making. Fear in and of itself is not the problem; it's your reluctance to admit vulnerability and try to rise above it that impedes breakthroughs in courage. The reward for courage is the self-confidence you develop by facing your fears and leading others forward into an uncertain future.

Be confident in decisions made at personal risk in service to the big picture. There may be bumps, bruises, and setbacks. You might not see benefits for a long time. But leaders' courageous actions define their greatness.

7

ACCOUNTABILITY

Who today will take the risk or blame
For someone else? Everyone is the same,
Dreading his neighbor's tongue or pen or deed,
Imprisoned in fear we stand . . .

—ANNE MORROW LINDBERGH (1906–2001)
(*The Unicorn and Other Poems*, Vintage: 1972)

"I am accountable. The buck stops with me." These are powerful words for a leader. What do they really mean?

Accountability means accepting responsibility for your choices, regardless of the consequences. It means owning up to your own character and conduct and recognizing the impact it has on others. To be accountable means that you are willing to admit to and learn from mistakes and foster a culture that allows others to try, fail, and get back up again. With accountability, you seek the truth and encourage others to do the same.

Accountability encourages humility and forgiveness for yourself and others. And for leaders, accountability extends beyond the self. In a commitment to the big picture, leaders are also responsible for the circumstances and conditions of their organizations. Whatever reality leaders face on their watch and under their supervision, it is up to them to accept it or change it, to take account and do something.

When the stakes are high and the specter of failure is hard at your heels, do you have the courage to admit your mistakes and learn from them? Can you be a leader who is brave enough to accept the responsibility for the consequences of your choices and decisions? Do you accept the responsibility for the big picture of your organization?

IT'S SO EASY TO BLAME

It's so easy to react to mistakes and wrongdoings with blame and judgment. But to what purpose? As the one in charge, you must rise above pettiness and finger-pointing. It is your job as the leader to accept and assess challenges, to rise above the easy path of blame, and to take the high road of truth and accountability.

Imagine the consequences if a pilot reacted to an in-flight mechanical failure with blame, accusation, or name-calling. At 35,000 feet, when an engine goes out, it would be disastrous for the pilot to do anything besides troubleshoot the problem and decisively determine the solution, using all available resources to get everyone safely down. This same level of accountability is fundamental to effective leadership.

Imagine the positive consequences if political leaders listened to, acknowledged, and respected opposing ideologies! Imagine the rate of political progress we could achieve if the rhetoric of blame were replaced with accountability. A culture of accountability that frowns upon blame would transform politics and business into progressive, positive, and creative institutions.

Accountability starts with you. As you read this chapter, I challenge you to throw down the mantle of blame and refrain from engaging in those conversations.

START BY ADMITTING MISTAKES

We all make mistakes. It's how you handle your mistakes and the mistakes made by others under your authority that determines accountability. When you courageously own up to your own shortcomings, it is a powerful demonstration of your common humanity. Others will rally behind you and be more willing to forgive you if you are honest, willing to take the hit, willing to learn from your mistakes, and willing to seek solutions. However, don't confuse proactive and authentic admissions of mistakes with a guileless, manipulative "woe is me." That's not accountability; that's the rationalization of a victim mentality. We see plenty of that in public lamentations and shallow apologies for unbelievably bad behavior on the part of high-profile people.

The same principles of honesty and authenticity apply when others make mistakes under your watch. Do you allow them to admit to their mistakes without fear of judgment? Do you provide an atmosphere that says it's okay to fall down, as long as you don't stay down? When mistakes are made, are others encouraged to figure out what went wrong, make corrections and amends, and move forward with better solutions?

Beware of those who use admissions of failure and weakness as a cover-up for taking responsibility. True accountability is built from honesty and sincerity combined with an intention to make things better. Be sure to draw a distinction between those who are seeking to improve and those who are happy to wallow in the satisfaction of being wrong and helpless. It is important to face mistakes and failure, but don't stop there. Accountability includes the next step of looking for the upside and learning from your mistakes.

DO YOU KEEP YOUR PROMISES?

When you agree to something, do you consistently deliver? Every time you break a promise, your effectiveness as a leader diminishes. Your level of authority is commensurate with your level of dependability. Accountability is as important in the simple things as it is in weightier commitments. When you tell someone you will call them back and don't, return an e-mail and don't, review the report and get back to them tomorrow and don't . . . your authority and credibility erodes, and others decide that you cannot be counted on. Accountability means that when you say you will do something, you do it, or if circumstances dictate that a change in plans is needed, you clearly communicate that and make another plan.

Small infractions of accountability go on all the time in organizations. In my younger CEO days, I only returned phone calls that I felt were important, and I made no arrangements for the others to be acknowledged in any way. I rationalized this by telling myself that I had a big job, and the weight of my responsibility superseded requests and queries that weren't on my priority list. Many years later, I put in a call to a busy CEO with a personal request. She didn't know me well and I didn't really expect that she would return the call. Much to my delight, she promptly called back. In our conversation I thanked her for that small gesture, which was very meaningful to me. She informed me that she returned every e-mail and every phone call in a timely manner, either personally or with administrative assistance. On reflection I realized how many people I had let down, how my lack of accountability to the small responsibility of returning phone calls must have left doubts in the minds of many about my dependability and character.

You might rationalize small infractions of accountability, but it's not worth it; being impeccable with your word is worth the reward of being seen by others as a leader they can depend on.

Needless to say, accountability for large indiscretions, for obvious failures under your watch, is even more important. It is always refreshing to hear political leaders say that they take responsibility. One of the best examples I witnessed was Akio Toyoda, the CEO of Toyota, taking responsibility on national TV for defects in his product. He went on to make a public commitment to listen and be responsive to customer complaints. He didn't have to do that; he could have delegated it to the PR department. He certainly didn't have to face Congress or go on national television. But he did. He has a firm handle on accountability.

I SHALL NOT TELL A LIE

Where does accountability come from, and how is it developed? Like so many essential leadership values, it takes shape in childhood.

When children make mistakes, they are faced with three choices: they can admit their mistake, blame someone else, or tell a lie. Depending on the severity of the consequences or a reconciliatory lesson from a loving adult, children learn to either hide the truth under blame or lies, or admit the truth, take their punishment, and learn from their mistakes. When children grow into adults, they take their learned behaviors with them into the workplace.

Consequently, there are leaders who move into adulthood with a mature sense of accountability, who accept the consequences of honesty.

Then there are those who learned to blame others for their failures, who continue to relinquish personal responsibility, and in doing so lose the opportunity to make amends and seek improvement.

At the extreme there are leaders who got away with lying and learned to be comfortable with it as a coping skill. These are the leaders who can't be trusted.

As a leader, you must belong to the first category. Be a mature adult who takes responsibility for your character and conduct and its impact on the world around you, in particular the world under the influence of your leadership.

FAILURE AS OPPORTUNITY

As a leader, when you face failures and setbacks, you must ask yourself: What can I do to make things better? How can I improve this situation? How can I contribute? How can I learn from my mistakes? How can I collaborate for unique solutions? The effect on the future of our world, if we were all accountable, would be extraordinary.

It should not be a stretch for leaders to own up to their mistakes, take responsibility for the condition of their institutions, and accept responsibility for the morale of their employees, the conduct of their teams, and the defects and failures of their products and services. It shouldn't be a tall order, but a brief Internet search of just one day's headlines on accountability in politics and business yields a different picture:

- Coach denies allegations of wrongdoing in sex/recruitment scandal.
- Church officials deny knowledge of sex abuse in parish.
- Senator not held accountable for accepting bribe.
- Lack of accountability threatens UN peacekeeping mission in the Congo.
- Incompetence of surgeons covered up in heart baby ordeal.

I found these disturbing headlines in two minutes; there are hundreds, if not thousands more on any given day. Everywhere you look, you can find hard-to-believe stories of blame, dishonesty, and lack of account-ability on the part of elected officials, CEOs, sports figures, and others in leadership positions.

When Lehman Brothers collapsed in September of 2008, it took with it approximately $629 billion in investor and company assets. There were executives at Lehman who knew that significant and potentially damaging risks were being taken that were not disclosed. Moody's, an industry watch-dog, was a significant partner in the brazen lack of accountability that pre-ceded the collapse. With full knowledge that over $50 billion of liability had been removed from the balance sheets under the auspices of a tactic called Repo 105 (a legal, but unethical, accounting gimmick to hide debt and increase cash), Moody's had given Lehman a AA rating only one week prior to the collapse. It would not have taken a genius to know that Lehman had been and was continuing to go down a dangerous path of excessive risk with marginalized transactions of derivatives and other nebulous instru-ments. But no one stood up and took responsibility—not the CEO, not the board, not the SEC. And when the house of cards inevitably came tumbling down, its CEO, Richard Fuld, blamed the markets. His law-yers asserted that Fuld didn't know what Repo 105 was. If he truly didn't know, he should have owned up to the fact that he wasn't competent to run Lehman. If he did know, then he was lying. Either way, as CEO he was responsible for and should have been accountable to the gross lack of oversight at his firm.

Fuld's poor leadership exemplifies the widespread lack of accountabil-ity that plagues leadership today. This behavior sends the message that it's okay to fail at the expense of others. Fuld and those associated with him are not going hungry personally, yet their lack of accountability has inflicted pain and hardship on millions of people.

The same thing is going on in politics, in corporations large and small, in for-profit and nonprofit organizations all over the world. This disas-trous trend needs to stop, and the change must start at the top. As leaders, we set the standards. As a leader, accountability means knowing that, in the end, the buck stops with you. You hired the person who is causing personnel problems; you can fire him. You delegated that project to a team not up to the task; you can reassign. Product defects? Low ratings on your employee satisfaction survey? Take responsibility and find a solution. In the face of these and other problems, you can react with anger and blame, or you can say, "I am accountable. What went wrong, and how can we make this better?" What a difference accountable leaders can make in the progress of our society!

THE HIGH PRICE OF BLAME

Too many leaders shirk accountability, choosing to hide behind blame (someone else is responsible) or feigned ignorance (I don't know who's responsible, but it's definitely not me). Fearing for their survival, many leaders fail to account for things going wrong under their watch. What is lost when leadership is not accountable? What do we lose when we don't take responsibility for our actions, our conduct, our relationships, our lives? We lose nothing less than the truth.

When responsibility is thwarted and replaced with the quick fix of blame, the full spectrum of the truth is obscured. We cannot learn from our mistakes, or right any wrongs, without the truth. No one benefits from blame; we all lose. We lose the opportunity to respect different perspectives, and we lose the chance to find unique and novel solutions to the most stubborn problems. When we resort to blaming others for the ills of our lives, our enterprises, and even the world, we are relinquishing responsibility to do something differently. When we cover up unintended and negative consequences, when we try to hide the truth of our lives and conduct, we limit our chances to become better people and better leaders. An accountable leader will not be afraid to own up to her mistakes, regardless of whatever consequences arise.

I once contracted for a short stint as a "loaner CEO" for a nationally recognized hospitality firm. They had acquired a small organization that was suffering from a series of leadership failures and poor decision making. In the month prior to my arrival, the general manager and all but one of the key managers had left. Joining their exodus was a league of key customers, top performers, and any remnant of positive employee morale.

As I climbed the stairs to the executive offices on my first day, I noticed an odd black thing leaning against the wall in the hallway. Curiosity piqued, I approached the object. It was the dirtiest, blackest air-conditioning filter I had ever seen. A strange thing to run into on my first day, but I soon realized it held the key to some of the major causes of the organization's precipitous decline in fortunes.

This ailing company was on its third owner in a four-year period, which had also included three acquisitions. The current owner had bought the company because it was cheap; a good deal. The new owner's primary initiative was to make the profit margins bigger. They aggressively pushed for more revenue, squeezing the expense side of the income statement to achieve results; but you can't squeeze blood out of a turnip. The previous two owners had seen to that.

A few months before my arrival, corporate had sent two of their youngest and brightest financial stars to spend a couple of days onsite. Their mission: make the numbers work. With a couple strokes of a pen, they obliterated two critical line items: quality control and, with it, a significant number of maintenance personnel. With no knowledge of the company's actual operations, the people involved, or the possible consequences of their decisions, these two financial analysts changed the numbers, got a sign-off from home base, and left. They did a fine job on paper, but in reality, they dealt a deathblow to an already weak and sinking ship.

Eliminating the simple but critical quality control and maintenance task of regularly checking and replacing air filters in hundreds of expensive properties resulted in clogged filters and associated equipment failure. Associated costs included the expense of replacing hundreds of whole-house systems. Hot and aggravated vacationers complained to unattended voice mail. Resigned and burned-out skeleton maintenance crews tried to stay under the radar, more intent on holding on to their benefit packages than risking notice by speaking out about quality control failures.

Within a month of that visit from corporate, most of the management team had left, unable to operate effectively under strategies and financial constraints that they knew wouldn't work. They had voiced their concerns, but to no avail. The result was a steep and steady decline in company revenues.

Once the management team had jumped ship, it was easy to place the blame on them, and that is what happened. The hierarchy of executive leadership ignored the part that they had played in the financial fallout resulting from decisions made without context or an awareness of consequence.

I put that grimy air filter front and center in the entrance to the executive offices. I wanted it to be a lasting symbol of the consequences of that fateful stroke of a pen on their financial planning document.

Where are the dirty air filters in your organization? What problems and hidden truths are being obscured by a lack of accountability? Persistent employee complaints, turnover, product defects, low morale? All could be pointing to a lack of accountability in your company's management structure. Even something as simple as burned-out light bulbs or an employee break area that is rarely cleaned can signal accountability issues. Look underneath the surface; problems can't be hidden forever. They will show up sooner or later, and you can be sure that later will not be better.

Look for the dirt under your own fingernails, and then look for the dirt in the organization. When things go wrong and you don't get the results you wanted, start with yourself before you seek to blame others. Ask questions: What went wrong here? Did I not give my staff what they needed? Were my expectations clear? Then take account, assume responsibility, clean it up, and move on.

TOOLS OF ACCOUNTABILITY

There is no structure or governing organization that defines and regulates leadership accountability. Leaders do not have a universally accepted code of conduct or ethics. Leadership accountability is largely a personal choice, a choice of conscience.

There are efforts afoot to implement MBA codes in business schools, as discussed in *The MBA Oath* by Max Anderson and Peter Escher, and there are ongoing discussions about making leadership a true profession, like those in "Why Management Must Be a Profession" by Harvard Business School professor Rakesh Khurana. But for the most part, accountability for the morale, vibrancy, and success of an organization rests with the character and moral makeup of each individual leader. Every leader has to make the choice to demonstrate accountability and to instill a culture of accountability in their organizations.

Is it important to you? Do you choose to foster a culture of truthfulness, a culture that recognizes the importance of being able to try and fail and then get up again? Or have you chosen to take the easy road of blaming and passing the buck? You can find the answer to these questions in the conversations of your employees. Listen.

PERFORMANCE ASSESSMENT

There are structures and systems available to support and encourage workforce accountability. Two that are widely used and recognized are the performance appraisal and the 360 review. A key responsibility for leaders is to nurture and develop others. Everyone can benefit from being held accountable to agreed-upon expectations and performance metrics. And no matter how self-motivated we are, we all can benefit from constructive feedback and structures to remind us of our responsibilities.

Yet in this important arena of performance management, many leaders, managers, executives, and CEOs, when faced with a performance problem, shy away from potential conflict or contentiousness. Performance appraisal systems may be in place, but they are met with great resistance. Instead of a transparent, honest, and constructive assessment of staff members' performance, many leaders hastily fill in the blanks and minimize communication with the recipient. Others elect to complain about their underperforming employees, write down notes in an employee file, never shared with the employee in question, and build a case to make the person in question "wrong" without ever having a frank discussion with them. This lack of accountability in performance appraisal systems invites backlash and lawsuits.

The 360 review is an invaluable tool for getting confidential and specific feedback from a range of peers, direct reports, and superiors. Conducted in a professional environment under professional, unbiased direction, the 360 review can provide leaders with examples of how their conduct is received and give them an opportunity to see things about themselves from outside perspectives. The 360 is a great mirror. Many leaders are happy to have these conducted on others but leave themselves out of the process, which of course is no way to show individual accountability. If you haven't participated in a 360 review, I encourage you to initiate one.

Morale, trust, and productivity are increased in organizations where staff members can count on transparency and feedback—be it good or bad. What counts is that they know that they will be held accountable, and that they will be given a chance to take responsibility for their actions and recover from mistakes.

MR. NICE GUY

During my many years of executive coaching, it has been a recurring frustration for me to watch people in key leadership positions allow the poor performance of one individual to negatively affect an entire organization.

A few years back, my consulting company was called in to clean up a personnel mess left by a temporary contracted CEO. Not having the best interests of the organization at heart, the CEO not only turned a blind eye to the poor performance of a key department head, he gave that department head an "A" evaluation and a big raise the week before he left, which meant that both the organization and the employee himself had an inflated opinion of his performance. The temp CEO chose not to be accountable for the effect that the department head's poor performance had had on his department, nor did the CEO take any responsibility for the resulting damage to the employees and their morale.

Instead, the temp CEO wanted to be the nice guy, to not make waves during his short tenure. He had no interest in confrontation or conflict. Rather than risk the possibility of a contentious performance discussion with an unhappy employee, he walked away—or rather he drove away in his expensive sports car—headed to his next highly paid, largely unaccountable adventure in leadership.

A leader should never allow one person to operate to the detriment of the whole organization—even if it means risking your own career status by confronting the issue head-on. Leaders are ultimately accountable to the big picture, a responsibility that supersedes any one individual's poor performance.

SURVEYS

Accountability extends beyond individual behavior for leaders. Looking at your organization, department, or whatever entity you are responsible for, what do you see? Step back and look. Pay attention to the overall character and morale of the people who work under your watch. Do you see commitment, enthusiasm, loyalty, excellence, productivity, and respect? Or do you see apathy, mediocrity, turnover, backstabbing, anger, and declining indicators? Leaders need to be able to accurately assess the overall morale and satisfaction of the people who work for them in order to effectively take responsibility for the culture and the health of their organizations.

If you are committed to providing a superior environment for employees and a superior product or service for customers, you need good feedback. An easy way to assess the morale and satisfaction of these two essential groups is through the use of surveys. The value of a survey comes from how well it is designed, how unbiased the reporting is, and how the results are used. Every endeavor should have some type of regular feedback mechanism. For small companies, a confidential in-house survey usually suffices. For larger institutions, hiring a professional service is the way to go.

Conducting the survey and receiving the results is only the first step. Then you must communicate the results, address the issues, and take proactive steps to make improvements. If your staff and your customers know that you value their input and are willing to address concerns and take steps to make things better, they will feel valued and will respond with loyalty.

I DIDN'T DO IT

What if you really *aren't* in any way responsible for the problems? What if you've inherited someone else's mess? Sometimes leaders step into a new position and are faced with a dysfunctional, broken, and divided organization. In those cases, it doesn't matter whose fault it is; as the leader, you are still accountable. It comes with the job. If you inherit a mess, a good start is to convey honesty and transparency about the condition of the company or department—not a judgment, but an honest assessment of your observations. This assessment and its accompanying communication should be followed by a collaborative development and clear articulation of a new vision with the inclusion of company values, all supported by a strategic plan.

The buck stops with you.

Take a good look around you. What you see is a reflection of your leadership. Do you like what you see? What are you willing to risk to make things better? When you are accountable, others will follow your lead.

RISING ABOVE THE FLIGHT OF FAILURE

There have been plenty of times in my career when telling the truth was like a painful and difficult tooth extraction.

Even so, "And the truth shall set you free" is one of my favorite sayings.

Leadership accountability is an important attribute for individual growth and development, and it is also the portal that enables us to move beyond failure. As difficult as it can be to admit fault, and as scary as the possible consequences are, I have always discovered important insights from my failures and learned from my mistakes. A good dose of humility is a great tonic for leaders from time to time.

I had a good dose of humility in 1997, when I was president of SouthEast Air, and also a member of the flight team.

In the 1990s aviation was a largely male-dominated profession, and still is. As a rule, pilots are independent, competitive, somewhat stoic guys. Admissions of failure are seldom heard. Instead of experienced and seasoned veterans sharing their mistakes and providing others with opportunities to avoid the same errors, the norm is to hide mistakes and not admit weaknesses.

David B. Lehr, better known as "Cap'n Dave," held the critically important position of Director of Operations at my small airline, and he was also a longtime pilot at TWA, flying intercontinental flights between the United States, Rome, and Honolulu in a 747. He and his wife Joyce lived waterfront on the Outer Banks, and he commuted to St. Louis for his TWA flight assignments. When he was home, he enjoyed heading out to our small regional airport and supporting us. He was an incredible asset to our start-up, bringing with him decades of experience as a pilot well acquainted with the FAA rules and regulations and the protocol of commercial air service.

With the weight of the responsibility that came with the position of director of operations, he had to pass regular exams by the FAA, which included observing how he instructed other pilots, both in the classroom and in the cockpit. So when he asked for a volunteer "subject pilot" to go with him to an FAA exam, I readily agreed. He was, after all, a critical member of the airline, and I wanted to support him as best I could.

At that point, I was still a relative newcomer to the world of commercial pilots. I knew little of the nuances of FAA Flight Reviews. When I told the other pilots I had volunteered, they reacted with a strange lack of enthusiasm and unwillingness to comment. I had expected high fives and maybe some advice from those with experience as subject pilots; instead I got nothing but dubious looks. I figured that perhaps I was more confident than they were, or maybe David thought I was a really good pilot. Or perhaps I was just more generous with my time than they were when it came to helping David.

For the exam, David and I had to go to the regional FAA office in Winston-Salem. On the day of the appointed check ride, we flew out in my Cessna 182. We enjoyed the flight and didn't spend much time talking about the upcoming test. The inspector was Mike Harville, an imposing man with a stoic demeanor and a formidable presence. Without much small talk, he ushered us into a conference room and began going down a list of aeronautical and aircraft-related questions for David and me. Harville was assessing how well David had trained me, so my answers were critical to David's success in the review. David had a great depth of knowledge of aviation rules and regulations, and maybe he felt that would be enough for this part of the exam. I certainly had done nothing to prepare. I was literally along for the ride. We did okay on this classroom portion, though not at all impressive.

The next part was the flight test. I had never flown with an FAA examiner before, so I was calm, but I sensed that David was apprehensive. His commercial airline career depended on the successful completion of FAA check rides, and he was not at all interested in having that jeopardized by a check ride in a Cessna with a low-time commercial pilot and an examiner in the backseat. He didn't share these concerns with me, though. At the time, I had no idea of the impact this flight could have on his career.

I was about to discover why none of the other pilots had agreed to go with David. What I had mistaken for a lack of confidence or time on their part was really inside knowledge of the inherent career risks of being the subject pilot on a FAA check ride: FAA examiners often find it easier to fail the subject pilot (me) than to fail the test pilot (David).

Up we went in my little Cessna, Harville in the backseat with a clipboard, David in the co-pilot seat, and naïve me at the controls. David was evaluating me, and Harville was evaluating David evaluating me. The first thing I learned was that check rides are excruciatingly quiet. The examiner watches in silence, taking notes, as the subject pilot is directed through maneuvers and in-flight challenges by the test pilot. If the subject pilot moves toward error or mistake, no one says anything. The examiner waits to see how far the pilot will go before she catches herself. Commercial pilots are trained to be alert, ready, and responsive to emergencies and breakdowns. If a pilot errs, the mistake is allowed to go on until the examiner feels like everyone's life is at risk. Up to that point—silence.

Part of my check ride that day included a simulated engine failure and the resulting decisions of where and how to land safely. I picked a touchdown spot that I thought would work and glided down to within a few hundred feet. Once I had pulled up and regained altitude, David noted that there was a small airport nearby that I would have reached if I had chosen it. He suggested that maybe that would have been a better choice. Okay, feedback noted. I completed a few more maneuvers, and the check ride was done. It was time to head back, land, and discuss the results. I thought I had done really well. Silence continued on the flight back and all the way to the airport reception area. Harville and David left me and went to his office to discuss the check ride.

When they finally emerged, they had another FAA inspector with them. Everyone seemed very serious. Harville cleared his throat and then said he was sorry, but I had failed the check ride. "Failure" was not something I heard often, especially in the arena of performance, whether piloting, running a business, academics, or sports. I could hardly hear the rest of what he said. David piped in, and the two of them gave rationales for their decision, but all I heard was "failure, failure, failure."

I was dazed, too shocked to say anything lest it come out in an angry tirade. I kept quiet except to say thank you, with a clenched jaw. My mind was busy judging those three men, making them wrong: *They're a bunch of chauvinists . . . Who do they think they are anyway . . . I'm smarter than they are . . .* On and on went this internal tirade. I was relieved when we shook hands and got out of there.

Once David and I were alone, flying back to the Outer Banks, I unleashed a frenzy of blame. What the hell was he talking about? That simulated emergency landing wasn't the best, but in my unhumble opinion it certainly didn't warrant failure. David listened to my furious rant, and then he explained the system: it was better to fail me for my bad decision than for him to fail his examiner test for a bad decision in not failing me. Because if *he* had failed the exam, it would have jeopardized his job flying to Rome; whereas my failure, though a serious blow to my ego, had little impact on my livelihood or future. I was, first and foremost, a businesswoman and CEO; a career as a commercial pilot was not something I was aiming for. *He* was the one being assessed; he was the one that the FAA was passing or failing based on how well I flew under his direction. For that reason, he was holding me to the highest standards, and he was not going to let anything slip by or put himself in a position where the FAA could say, "You should have failed her because . . . "

So I had been little more than a guinea pig. And more important, I had failed a check ride.

I tried to blame David. I tried to blame the FAA. I tried to blame sexism. But it didn't work. I had failed, period. With a good night's sleep and a clearer head, I decided to swallow my pride and take full responsibility. The next day I apologized to David for my outburst. I told the team about my failure. I vowed to become an even better pilot. I practiced emergency landings. I became more proficient. I gained a new appreciation for the contribution David made to our small airline. I ratcheted up my own professionalism and insisted on the same from the other pilots. As a team, we got sharper and held ourselves to higher standards. I took that failure and the lessons it offered and incorporated them into building a better company and raising the standards for the whole flight team.

I drank a stiff dose of the tonic of humility. Yet owning my mistake had the opposite effect of what I'd feared. Instead of losing credibility with the other pilots, with my accountability came a newfound respect.

I will make mistakes, again and again. But now I know that the more accountable I am, the better prepared I'll be to take on the challenges of my life and career, to accept them without blame or judgment. Over the years, I have become ever more forthright about my failures as well as my successes.

A few years ago, I made a trip to Paris. While there, I met up with my mother and a friend of hers who were there for a Kiwanis Club exchange program. As we strolled down a café-lined boulevard, her friend inquired about my background and past. When I began to share one of my stories, my mother interrupted with, "Don't tell her that." For a brief moment I was not on that Parisian street but back in the small airport reception area, learning that I had failed at something that was really important to me. Having learned the value of life's hard lessons, I said to my mother, "If she doesn't know about my failures as well as my successes, she can't really understand me."

Accountability begins with our own lives, the good and the bad. It is in those dark and messy moments that the integrity of our character is built, our courage is inflamed, and our capacity to handle life's challenges is forged. With this wisdom, we become more adept at maneuvering through a world filled with unexpected disappointments, a world that throws curveballs, a world that will always be imperfect, despite our best efforts. We become the person that people want and deserve to have as their leader. They want to believe in us through thick and thin, in good times and bad, in success and failure. When we are accountable to our important role in the world, as leaders and as individuals, we begin to have the capacity to move mountains.

ACCOUNTABILITY

To appreciate accountability, start by identifying who and what you blame. Then shift your mindset from blaming to proactively taking responsibility and seeking solutions.

I. **Moving Beyond Blame**

Identify a person, a work situation, an external factor, or a self-limitation that you blame for holding you back. Can you change the cause of your frustration?

A person (describe who/why): _____

_____

Can you change him or her? YES ___ NO ___

A work situation (describe it): _____

_____

Can you change it? YES ___ NO ___

An external factor (for example, the economy, politics, weather, competition): _____

_____

Can you change it? YES ___ NO ___

A self-limitation (for example, weight, time, age, education): _____

_____

Can you change it? YES ___ NO ___

For each yes, write down what you can do to effect change:

Person _____

Work situation _____

External factor _____

Self-limitation _____

Where you answered no, it means that you are spending time and energy blaming or worrying about someone or something that you can't change or control. What you can do in those situations is to step away from blame, take action, or change your attitude. For example, if you don't like your boss, you can't fire him, and you can't change him. So what can you do? You can leave the job or decide that you will look for the positive in him and eliminate negativity and blame from your internal and external conversations.

Blaming things and people out of your control is a waste of your precious time and a diversion from taking responsibility. Rather, constantly shift your focus to creative problem solving and solution seeking.

II. **Shouldering Blame and Dealing With Failure**
Below are some questions relating to failure and mistakes. As you answer the questions, listen to your inner voice and be aware of your gut feelings. Those indicators will tell you where you need to focus attention.

Circle the response that best describes you:

I admit to failures.

Often   Sometimes   Seldom   Never

I learn from failure.

Often   Sometimes   Seldom   Never

I admit my mistakes.

Often   Sometimes   Seldom   Never

I say I'm sorry when I'm wrong.

Often   Sometimes   Seldom   Never

I hold myself to a high standard of accountability.

Often   Sometimes   Seldom   Never

Others can count on me to be accountable.

Often   Sometimes   Seldom   Never

As a leader, you are held to higher standards for personal and organizational accountability. If you are uncomfortable with failure and tend to hide your mistakes, you need to work to overcome that tendency and learn the value of accountability.

III. Creating a Culture of Accountability

    A. Identify someone you work with who is incessantly complaining and blaming.

        Who and what (describe):

        _____

        _____

        Have a nonjudgmental but direct conversation with this person about blame, accountability, and taking responsibility. Share this chapter with her. Encourage her to brainstorm proactive solutions to the issue.

    B. Inform your staff that from now on, you will not discuss problems with them unless they have solutions. Let them know that blaming others is no longer acceptable. From now on you want to hear solutions. Stick to it. Give immediate feedback when you hear people complaining about the same thing over and over. Create a culture of accountability.

Blame, judgment, denigration, and condemnation are not good tools for a leader who desires to grow and contribute. Accountability is an essential leadership attribute for overcoming persistent barriers, resolving long-standing conflicts, and creating new solutions to old problems.

6

POSSIBILITY

Aviation is proof that given the will, we have the capacity to achieve the impossible.

—EDDIE RICKENBACKER (1890–1973),
CEO of Eastern Airlines and WWI Ace of Aces

As far back as the sixteenth century, Leonardo da Vinci dreamed of flight, saying, "For once you have tasted flight, you will walk the earth with your eyes turned skyward, for there you have been and there you will long to return." Four hundred years later, the Wright brothers took that dream and turned it into reality. They were convinced that it was possible, and they were right. What we think shapes what we do. Impossible or possible is an internal conversation that constantly directs our choices and colors the outcomes. Our minds powerfully influence the design of our lives.

An individual's ability to perceive and conceive beyond what is taught and acquired and venture into the realm of possibility provides the substance of humanity's advancement from survival to innovation.

A leader who faces challenges with a strong belief in possibility is a leader who moves beyond what has been to what can be. A leader's ability to push indoctrination, convention, and limited perceptions out of the way to make room for new product ideas, different organizational structures, and innovative strategies is often the determinant of which organizations make it and which fall by the wayside. A leader can be an organization's source of inspiration and possibility, or he can be its death.

THE ARCHITECTURE OF POSSIBILITY

Embracing possibility means using our capacity to think outside of our own limited beliefs and experiences. It is the ability to engage in and encourage out-of-the-box thinking—or, in aviation terms, to push the envelope, to break the sound barrier, to fly across uncharted oceans, to be the first to walk on Mars. Possibility is an inner spark of wonder and boundless curiosity. It imagines a world of potential solutions to challenges and obstacles, instead of a world constrained by convention and what has always been. To live by the principle of possibility is to believe there are alternatives that might not be in your realm of conscious understanding.

Possibility was what my father's best friend offered when, as a young woman, I was considering the nontraditional route of obtaining an MBA and becoming a businesswoman. In the culture I grew up in, women pretty much stayed home and men worked. Defying convention, I had decided to apply for admission to graduate business school. At a Christmas party that year, my dad's friend, one of the most successful business owners in town, pulled me aside. He told me about his family business, how they had started from scratch and now had a large chain of stores. He said, "Betty, you are head and shoulders above the guys when it comes to brains and gumption. You go for it." His words excited my imagination and opened my eyes. In that brief moment of mentoring, he allowed me to rise above the naysayers and small-town judgment to envision a future filled with possibility. Maybe I would start my own business some day! Or perhaps I would have an office in New York or Boston? I could feel the excitement of financial freedom. He opened my eyes to the possibility of exciting new frontiers.

If my father's friend's words can have such impact, imagine the effect leaders can have when they recognize what is possible in others and in their organizations.

POSSIBILITY CAN CHANGE THE FUTURE

In 1992, the Currituck County, North Carolina, commissioners voted to buy a historic but long-neglected hunting lodge called the Whalehead Club in Corolla, North Carolina. The commissioners believed that preserving and protecting this landmark was not only an important part of the heritage of the community but it also could serve to protect and increase the valuable tourist market that kept county schools and services well funded. But there was strong disagreement from mainland locals who didn't want their tax dollars invested in a dilapidated building two hours away in a remote coastal community. The vote was contentious. As a consequence, several of the commissioners lost their seats in the next election. Those leaders knew that their political careers were at stake when they cast their yes vote, but their willingness to stand for what was possible in the face of naysayers paved the way for one of the finest attractions on the Currituck Outer Banks. The majestic Whalehead Club has been carefully restored and attracts millions of visitors each year. It stands as an invaluable and intriguing piece of history from the old days of wealthy aristocrats, the sport of duck hunting and the local men and women who made it possible. The commissioners' belief in possibility resulted in a steady income stream of admission fees and concession sales, an important contributor to the financial health of the council.

BEWARE OF YOUR COMFORT ZONE

I, like so many people, am often tempted to stick with what makes me comfortable. After all, why change what's working? And certainly we should not change simply for the sake of change. I fight against complacency, because I know that the world awaits with a limitless array of choices and opportunities for my growth as an individual and for my attention to contributing beyond what is comfortable. Most of us have a natural tendency to preserve and protect, to take shelter in what's familiar. But leaders must be prepared to move beyond their comfort zones. Leaders need to constantly scan the horizon for competitive advantages and innovative opportunities.

Blockbuster was a major player in the movie rental business for decades, but the company failed to keep up with the changing technological landscape. In 2010 it filed for Chapter 11 and was delisted from the New York Stock Exchange. Blockbuster fell behind the power curve when it failed to keep up with the technologies of streaming introduced by wireless technology. On the other hand, Reed Hastings, the CEO of Netflix, sought new possibilities for his predominantly mail-order movie-rental business. He has led his company beyond the hard-copy DVD-rental model that served them so well and into online streaming and subscriptions. While Blockbuster continues to fade into obscurity, Netflix's stock price soared from $30 per share in 2009 to a high of $206 per share in 2010. One company stuck to the old, the other embraced possibility.

The publishing industry is facing challenge and change spurred on by advances in paperless technology. While some publishing leaders hold on to what they know and understand (the hardback book, the sales and marketing distribution structure, bookstores), others have jumped into the paperless world of Kindles and Nooks, print-on-demand, and social media promotion. The future will surely reward those who were willing to think beyond convention, to be inventive and embrace new possibilities.

Products and services are constantly under threat of obsolescence. In my lifetime I have witnessed the obsolescence of typewriters, turntables, mimeograph machines, eight-track players, cassettes, and albums just to name a few. I expect that the future will not be kind to gas-fueled cars, windup watches, e-mail accounts, hand-written letters, paper maps, hardback books and landlines.

Is there anything in your leadership purview that is threatened by obsolescence? What might be replaced by the emerging needs of tomorrow? What are the future challenges to your products and business? What is possible beyond what you know and are comfortable with?

It is critical that leaders have the ability to look beyond what is, to what is possible. We must combat our intellectual obsolescence and get outside of our comfort zone.

HOLDING OUT FOR THE RIGHT THING

Possibility is a powerful attribute for leaders to have in decision making, in the development of personnel and teams, and in facing crises. In all three areas, leaders often succumb to the allure of quick and willful snap decisions. When leaders are in volatile, rapidly changing circumstances and are faced with mounting pressure to make choices, they often don't take the time to explore different options or to solicit alternatives and possibilities. I have coached many executives who have personnel issues because they made a bad hiring decision thinking there weren't any good candidates. A hard truth is that it is a lot easier to hire than fire. Once you hire the wrong person, it can be incredibly difficult to correct the mistake.

Generally, I kindly point out it is improbable that in a world of 6.5 billion people there weren't *any* other qualified candidates. The usual response is, "I didn't have time." Executives have a lot of reasons for why something is not possible, when in reality what's holding them back or seemingly forcing them to compromise is not the lack of possibility but their own refusal to allow other possibilities to emerge.

Possibility thinking can be squelched by overload and by restricted access. It is as easy to be limited by what you think as it is to be overwhelmed by a seemingly endless flow of ideas and opinions. It certainly takes skill to balance the myriad possibilities available to you with your own set of limited beliefs and the need to be decisive and provide timely and definitive direction. How can possibility, practicality, and timeliness meet in the middle?

DEVELOPING POSSIBILITY THINKING

Although some people are born with natural curiosity, many leaders are weak and uncomfortable with the creative, intangible world of possibility. How can you incorporate its strengths and take advantage of its contribution to innovation?

Begin by surrounding yourself with a team of individuals who have diverse skills and experience and a shared commitment to the purpose and goals of your project. Solicit their divergent ideas and listen without judgment. Be aware of extremes and read as much as you can from broad points of view. Don't get shut down or sucked in by naysayers; rather, see their objections as highlighting areas that may need more attention.

When I introduced a new program called the Conch Club in one of my companies, there were plenty of naysayers. The new club invited homeowners to increase the appeal of their property through a comprehensive program that promised visitors beds made upon arrival, windows cleaned regularly, welcome gifts for weary travelers, on-the-spot carpet cleaning, and a whole array of services designed to lure and secure the best and the most vacationers. At the time, this was a big departure from the standard beach vacation rental model, where tourists brought their own linens, their own towels; many brought their own kitchen utensils. It had historically been a "we'll sweep up after ya" kind of business, a bring "everything but the kitchen sink" vacation model.

I didn't have all the details of how the Conch Club would actually work figured out, but I strongly believed in the possibilities it offered for the future of our company. The resisters gave me great insight into what needed to happen: "But who will make the beds?" "Where can you wash all those linens?" "There aren't any window cleaning companies." "The owners will never go for that!" All those objections opened the door to innovative solutions, and the wildly successful Conch Club became the standard-bearer for vacation rentals in the region.

Another thing a leader can do to unlock possibility is to recognize and accept that you operate from behind the clouded lens of your own limited perspective. Be aware that you have biases that can impede the emergence of other possibilities. Allow yourself to be open to suggestions from those brave enough to go against the grain. Learn to be comfortable with the discomfort of uncertainty, and take the time to allow nascent ideas to percolate. Listen to constructive criticism and objections; there are usually great ideas in there if you are nonjudgmental and can stop hearing only what you want to hear.

The success of my vacation real estate business was built on the back of customer complaints; our best ideas came from the customer surveys that we asked for and diligently responded to.

Recognize when you have become cynical, impatient, and stuck with a black-or-white approach to leadership. "It's my way or the highway," is an attitude that douses the spark of originality.

Stay curious about what you are inclined to immediately reject, what you are afraid of, and what you think is wrong. Challenge yourself to learn about opposing views or ideologies.

A PINK CADILLAC

One afternoon, in the very early days of my vacation rental company, when customers were few and far between, a pink Cadillac with gold spoke rims pulled into our tiny office in Kitty Hawk, North Carolina. Everyone stared. And when Alicia Vendani stepped out in her tight pedal-pusher pants, five-inch heels, and a leopard-print t-shirt, most of our jaws dropped open. With her was her mother-in-law, who was equally impressive, with the biggest platinum-blonde hairdo I have seen outside of Dolly Parton. Being a Southern-born and -bred doctor's daughter, these two inner-city Philadelphian women were definitely not my typical idea of potential second-home customers. But I pushed aside my gut reaction and chose instead to adopt an openness to possibility and a desire to engage with the unknown.

As it turned out, I never had more fun with a client than I did with Alicia. She was my first-ever real estate sale. She bought a house in a neighborhood I had no experience with, done by a builder I had never heard of. But I held on to possibility. At the closing, she showed up with a suitcase filled with cash. And if that wasn't enough, she'd brought me a gift: a pair of brightly colored, skintight pedal-pushers! With an open mind, anything seemed possible for this, my first-ever real estate sale.

THE RISK OF STICKING WITH WHAT YOU KNOW

The 2009 bankruptcies and slow reemergence of two of the United States' largest automakers, General Motors and Chrysler, are telling examples of leaders refusing to give up the old and embrace emerging possibilities. On the other hand, Toyota stayed ahead of the curve and geared up to deliver products that offered more cost-effective and efficient transportation possibilities.

The collapse and resulting weakening of our financial institutions has had a huge ripple effect on our businesses, our communities, our status in the world, and the lives of millions of individuals. Much of it can be traced back to executives' decisions to stubbornly hold on to producing, trading, and marketing products that held little to no value for the future needs of their constituents. Seduced by huge cash flow from financial instruments with little fundamental value, many turned their back on the future possibilities of their employees, organizations, and customers.

WINNING, OVERCOMING, AND REINVENTING

Possibility is at the heart of the success of athletic champions. When I have been the underdog in competitive sports, tired and worn out, the possibility of winning has been the fuel for actually being able to win. Possibility thinking is very powerful and can help you overcome seemingly overwhelming odds.

Sometimes leaders find themselves face-to-face with daunting challenges that defy conventional solutions and wisdom. At a World Forum presentation I attended, Rudy Giuliani described what it was like to be the mayor of New York City on 9/11. He shared with the audience that a leadership attribute he relied on heavily during those difficult days was possibility. He said that he constantly forced himself to ask himself and others, "What can we do? What are the possible solutions?" He kept fear at bay and stayed open to possibility, leading others to endure the unimaginable by providing a strong platform of leadership that said, "There is a way! We may not be able to see it now, but let's find it."

Possibility will keep an organization from aging and help it reinvent itself year after year, decade after decade, generation after generation. In 2008, Bill Ford, the forty-three-year-old CEO of Ford Motor Company, met with William McDonough, a renowned architect and the author of *Cradle to Cradle: Remaking the Way We Make Things*. The purpose of the meeting was to explore the possibilities for Ford's outdated, obsolete, and largely contaminated Rouge factory site, which, in its heyday, had been one of the most admired industrial complexes in the world. Together, these two men came up with the possibility of redesigning and reworking the factory, morphing it from an outdated assembly line to a model for twenty-first-century manufacturing, and creating the site for the production of the Model U, a cradle-to-cradle car built for environmental efficiency. The Model U will be powered by the world's first supercharged hydrogen internal combustion engine and equipped with a hybrid electric transmission and pioneering green materials and processes.

When technology and innovation threaten your business or product, don't spend time holding on; bring in new thinkers, promote out-of-the-box brainstorming, and let go of the thought of loss and replace it with possibility thinking. As Einstein said, "We can't solve problems by using the same kind of thinking we used when we created them."

POSSIBILITY THINKING

Tomorrow's problems will not be solved by yesterday's answers. Fresh perspectives and unprejudiced minds are critical for new solutions. The contributions and creative energy of younger generations are essential for changing paradigms and finding new answers. Possibility thinking is what created the iPod, the microchip, Google, and Facebook. It was the force behind peace in Ireland, the end to apartheid in South Africa, and the launchpad for putting a man on the moon. If leaders expect to create new products or find solutions to age-old conflicts and challenges, they must be willing to explore new worlds outside of their current line of sight.

Possibility is a valuable tool in a leader's arsenal. Don't underestimate its transformative and creative power because it has such a "soft" name, or because it doesn't show up in managerial handbooks or leadership courses. In the face of ultrachallenging circumstances—the discovery of fraud in your financial operations, the loss of a significant line of credit or a primary customer, the obsolescence of a bestselling product—ask how you can best lead under the circumstances, and work to discover what the possibilities are.

Leaders must stay ahead of the curve through the application and discipline of having an open mind, an attitude of resourcefulness, and a firm and steady belief in the vast array of potential solutions to the most stubborn of problems.

THE POSSIBILITY OF FLIGHT
AND RISING ABOVE THE IMPOSSIBLE

Inherent in the idea of flight are the feeling and the emotion of unlimited possibility. When you take control of an airplane for the first time, when you rise above an earthbound existence and add a set of wings to your life, the world of possibility opens up. On any given day, when I am challenged with problems, constraints, and conflict, a flight along the coastline of the Outer Banks of North Carolina can help me shift from unproductive worry into possibility thinking. It is from that frame of reference that I can move beyond my conventional thinking and allow my mind to wander into expansive and creative reverie.

Other great catalysts for possibility thinking have been those moments when I was told that something couldn't be done. In fact, some of my life's greatest ventures and adventures have been developed through the world of possibility generated by doors being slammed shut.

※

THERE'S A LITTLE FIGHTER PILOT IN ALL OF US

I grew up in a big house on a dead-end street in a conservative town in Virginia. There were sixteen families on the street, forty-two kids, and at one count over forty-five dogs. We were safe, we rode our bikes wherever we wanted, we walked long distances to school, and we had housekeepers. We had dads who worked all day and moms who stayed home or had small jobs for "pin money." As the third girl, I was raised to have good manners, to be well educated, well dressed, and well trained in social etiquette. The expectation was that I would be a housewife, a mother, and maybe take on a little side job from time to time, and of course that a man would provide for me, and I would stand behind him with support.

As I moved into my teen years, women's rights were starting to make waves. As a senior in high school, I watched on TV as women burned their bras in a bin on the boardwalk at Atlantic City in protest of the Miss America pageant. Birth control pills were suddenly on the market, allowing women a new sense of sexual freedom. Formerly all-male institutions were opening up their doors to let the girls in. I rolled into my twenties in an era that said discrimination is not okay and equal rights for men and women was a constitutional guarantee.

The newly paved road to gender equality was not a smooth one, however, and I was often a test driver. In 1982, I had just completed my MBA and was in the midst of job searching and all the challenges that face young adulthood. I decided to take a break and head home for a weekend of much-needed pampering and home-cooked meals. While there, my mother planned a picnic outing to a Blue Angels air show at our local airport, Preston Glenn. It was a crisp fall day with blue skies and a few high cirrus clouds. In those days, local airports were ungated and unguarded. The fields surrounding the runways were filled with people enjoying an afternoon of tailgating, camaraderie, and the thrill of the Blue Angels and their death-defying aerial maneuvers. Over 30,000 people showed up that fall day, spread their blankets, unpacked picnic baskets, and waited excitedly for the show to begin.

I staked out a spot on the blanket and allowed my mind to wander, regarding the shapes, sizes, and lifestyles of the people around me. And then out of the blue, I heard the deafening roar of the full throttles of a fighter jet and looked toward the sound. Two perfectly aligned F-18s roared over my head, followed in rapid succession by two more, and then two more. I climbed up onto the roof of the car to see better, mesmerized by the power, speed, and the measured daring of the Blue Angels. Snap rolls, barrel loops, diamond formations, wing-to-wing overlaps, contrails, and low-level flybys were performed with an exactness that defied gravity and brushed aside the specter of death. All the performances were accompanied by the *oohs* and *aahs* of the spectators and punctuated by thunderous applause. Watching in awe, I suddenly knew that I belonged up there with them, not bound to the earth with shoes and socks and measured steps, but up there in the sky.

As I continued to watch those pilots and their machines, I was busy piecing together the possibility of getting into the left seat of a fighter jet and taking control of the stick. Becoming more enmeshed in the vision of myself in a cockpit, I forgot all about my difficult job search and the other anxieties of my uncertain future. Then, I caught a glimpse of a small trailer on the edge of my peripheral vision, which I realized was a recruiting station for the Navy. I decided then and there that I would sign up to become if not a Blue Angel, then at least a fighter pilot.

I headed to the recruitment trailer, where I was greeted by a smiling Navy emissary. "I want to be a fighter pilot," I told him. He was intrigued and seemed genuinely interested; unbeknownst to me, he was motivated by minority recruiting goals, which included quotas for women. I asked about flight training, and he answered with a long explanation about maps and charts. I asked about the physical requirements of being a Navy pilot, and he talked about basic training and equal opportunity. I asked about the length of time it takes to fly solo, and he told me about teamwork and individual contribution to the missions. This back-and-forth eventually led him to explain that I would be perfect for a navigator position, an important position on the flight team. As a doctor's daughter, I had never heard of a navigator, so I listened intently as he described the support role of the navigator, who sits behind the pilots and attends to a complicated array of instrumentation and avionics. I was not hearing the words "fly" or "pilot."

"I don't want to navigate," I said. "I want to *fly*."

To which the recruiter responded, "Females can't be fighter pilots in the United States Navy."

Bam! The door was slammed shut, and my vision of being a Navy pilot at the controls of one of the most sophisticated planes in the world was erased. With a curt "No thanks," I headed out of the trailer, down the steps, and onto the field. I realized that I was being denied an opportunity simply due to my gender, but in that moment of impossibility, I embraced possibility and vowed that I *would* be a pilot. I didn't know how or when, but I made a commitment to myself that one day I would feel the power of a wide-open engine under my hand placed on a throttle.

That was in 1982. I took my first flight lesson in 1986 and obtained my private pilot's license in 1993. In 1994 I received my training as a commercial pilot, and I passed the test under the tutelage of Virginia Aviation at the very same airport where I'd seen the Blue Angels. From there I endured the long hours of instrument training, the frustrations of learning to fly with no visual references, flying and landing, and taking off under the hood. And finally, in 1998, I received the ATP rating, the top rating you can achieve in civilian aviation. To this day, there are less than nine hundred women in the United States with that rating.

Since that afternoon in 1982, I have flown over 2,500 hours in single-engine planes, in twin-engine Cessnas and sleek Pipers, and in executive-styled turboprops. I have yet to pilot a commercial or military jet, but I will. I'm not sure how, but I hold on to that possibility.

I believe there is a little fighter pilot in every leader. It's a voice inside of you that dares you to defy convention, to rise above the weight of the past and imagine a new future. What is your fighter pilot telling you about your potential? What is your fighter pilot telling you about the future of your organization? She is trying to tell you to look beyond the horizon, seek the vast expanses of possibility, break through the barriers of convention, and create something new, something different.

POSSIBILITY

The following exercises are designed to guide and support you in keeping possibility alive and well in your decision making and leadership conduct.

KEEPING POSSIBILITY ALIVE

I. Possibility Team

Each year, appoint a "possibility team" to come up with an innovative product, project, or operational change for your organization. Make it an honor to be on the team, and give the results exposure. Publicly recognize the new ideas that they contribute to the future well-being of the organization.

II. Back to Kindergarten

Go and speak to a kindergarten class. Ask the students what they want to do when they grow up or what their greatest wish is. You will witness possibility in its pure form. Take a little of the kindergartener back to work with you.

III. Think Different

Put something in your office that reminds you of possibility, like a picture or a quote that inspires you. For me, it's a black-and-white photo of Amelia Earhart with a caption that says "Think different." Do the same for your organization as a whole: post inspirational posters or quotes all around. Make sure they reflect the culture of the organization.

IV. Create the Right Atmosphere

The next time you have a meeting to discuss an issue that is difficult to resolve, start off with a brainstorming exercise like the one below. Encourage a free flow of ideas and possibilities:

1. Divide the group into small teams, making sure to pair people of divergent interests and opinions. Give the teams fifteen minutes to come up with five possible solutions with no qualifiers (fifteen minutes is enough time to be creative but not enough time to be overly analytical).

2. Instruct each team to present their five possibilities. List all the possibilities on a whiteboard.

3. Have the whole group choose three.

4. Divide into three larger teams and task each with analyzing one of the three chosen solutions, including its pros and cons, benefits and costs, and time and resources and to come up with recommendations.

5. Hold another meeting, present and discuss these possibilities. Seek consensus on a course of action.

V. **Step Away**

Consider whether you need to lift yourself out of your routine and clear your head by stepping away from analyses, opinions, and reports. If so, commit to taking a trip, attending a retreat, going on a hike, finding solitude, or stepping into a whole new world. Possibility thinking needs space in a busy brain—make room for it.

5

RESOLUTION

"Conceived by genius, achieved by dauntless resolution and unconquerable faith"

—INSCRIPTION ON THE WRIGHT BROTHERS MONUMENT,
Kitty Hawk, North Carolina

There are times when even the most outstanding leaders secretly wish it would all just go away—the challenges, the disappointments, the pressures, the endurance contest that is being a leader. Sometimes it just seems like you'll never get a break. The new product line you fought for persistently exceeds cost projections and misses targeted sales levels. The taskforce you assembled to address solutions to a vital competitive challenge can't seem to reach a conclusion. The talented new manager you lured away from the competition is creating more problems than he is worth. Second- and third-quarter results aren't coming close to your forecasts. It seems that no matter which way you turn, you encounter another problem, hit a dead-end, or face more delays.

Leaders are constantly faced with failure and disappointment. There are plenty of perks that often go with being the boss—more money, a bigger office, staff support, and a clear path for career advancement. But those take a backseat when you are facing an uphill struggle with no end in sight. In the face of setbacks, stalemates, and catastrophes, leaders are required to be constructive problem-solvers—even miracle workers. You are expected to keep going when all around you things are falling apart and people are quitting. You are expected to keep everyone else focused and on task, despite the obstacles and setbacks. You are expected to steadfastly persevere, bringing everyone else with you to the finish line.

What is it that allows great leaders to seek solutions, to continue to mobilize people toward accomplishment, to achieve results in the face of seemingly unending challenge? How do they do it?

They know the meaning and value of resolution.

Resolution is determination, tenacity, and perseverance. It allows a leader to overcome daunting obstacles and continue to seek solutions to complicated situations. It is a force that fuels athletes, executives, and legislators, compelling them to keep going until the race or endeavor is complete. It is an inner voice that says, "I will not give up."

In leadership, resolution leads to the successful completion of goals and strategies. It supports leaders in achieving their desired outcomes and delivering on their commitments.

CHILDHOOD LESSONS

One of the greatest and hardest lessons I learned as a child was to finish what I started. My mother was a stickler for details and a champion of completion. On any given Saturday morning, when my friends were gathered at the end of our dead-end street, preparing for the day's adventures, I was stuck in my house, finishing chores. One chore in particular sticks in my memory: cleaning the shower tiles with a toothbrush and Clorox. There were hundreds of little tiles. The task was a real challenge for a ten-year-old with an underdeveloped capacity to stay focused! But it taught me stick-to-itiveness that has served me well as an adult.

That Saturday morning shower stall task later helped me through many weeks of tough exams and term papers in college. Every business that I have created benefited from the strength of my resolve. When I feel overwhelmed and weighted down by the amount of sheer hard work, attention to detail, and looming deadlines that are part of every start-up, my resolve carries me through.

When I was a ten-year-old stuck cleaning the shower on Saturday mornings, I didn't particularly appreciate my mother. But I am certainly grateful today that she taught me discipline and perseverance, qualities that continue to support my resolution when I take on tough challenges.

FINISH WHAT YOU START

In leadership, resolution is the glue that holds together strategy and implementation. In a typical strategic-planning process, values are defined, vision is articulated, and a mission statement is produced. Strategies and goals are developed to support the future direction of the organization, complete with dates and metrics. Resolution is the ingredient needed to keep everyone's nose to the grindstone as they stretch their physical and intellectual limits, to finish what they started. One part determination and one part willpower, resolution is an engine of execution and accomplishment. Simply put, resolution is the ability to finish what you started.

In the absence of resolution, leaders too often give up on taking projects to conclusion, leaving those who put in the hard work increasingly cynical about the value of their efforts. "Flavor of the month," is an expression of frustration I have heard way too often in my role as consultant. This cynical comment speaks volumes about the underlying frustration in many organizations, where a lot of plans and programs never reach fruition. Hours of research and effort are wasted regularly, as leaders hop-skip from one thing to another in short spurts of interest, never truly resolving long-standing problems or recognizing the valuable input of others. Who can blame the staff for becoming cynical and disgruntled?

One of the most promising consulting projects in my career was the introduction and implementation of succession planning into a major healthcare institution. The CEO was planning for his upcoming retirement after a long and successful career with the organization. He wanted to ensure that he left behind a legacy that included a strong and well-prepared management team. Part of the project included facilitating the work of a team tasked with defining the attributes and skills that would best serve the future leadership needs of the organization. The team was also asked to develop a career ladder that would support the growth and development of aspiring and existing leaders. This team represented a cross section of the organization's most talented management staff members. They were really excited about defining the important topic of leadership at their place of work. I spent several months with this enthusiastic team of young executives on the development of these career ladders—which were never implemented. The team produced well-artic-ulated and thought-out descriptions of attributes that would elevate the cadre of leadership and set the standard for aspirants, but the lists that were presented were merely filed away.

The months of their passionate commitment and hard work on this project seemed wasted when a new CEO came on board. The resolve needed to implement the great ideas and plans for leadership develop-ment left with the outgoing CEO. The board's chosen successor had no interest in someone else's idea of leadership. The recommendations and plans of the team fell by the wayside, and along with it their excitement about the future of leadership at their organization. Within two years, more than half of that talented team had left.

When completion of a task is indefinitely postponed, people grow resigned and resentful of the fickleness of their leaders. When plans are dropped and initiatives shelved due to waning interest or diverted focus, those who did the work walk away with a feeling of hopelessness. When the efforts produced by long hours and hard work are abandoned on a dusty shelf, apathy creeps in and eats away at the remaining vestiges of passion and commitment. Sounds bad, doesn't it? Yet this is a com-monplace occurrence in many organizations. Finish what you start, and motivate others to do the same.

GIVE ME A BREAK!

Burnout can sneak up on you and obscure your ability to clearly see a way through difficulty. When you are worn out and on the brink of quitting, you need to find a way to recharge your batteries.

When I take on a start-up, I know from experience that I will face long hours, day after day of hard work, and a steady stream of challenges and problems that need solutions *now*. So part of my start-up plans include taking five days off every two months. I know that I need to get away from my e-mails, my BlackBerry, and my iPad long enough to get a fresh outlook on whatever is ahead. I let everyone know that this is going to happen; it is on my to-do lists and on my calendar.

Leaders need physical stamina and mental clarity for the long run. This is true for pilots as well. Fatigue and burnout are real dangers to pilots, who must be strong and alert in the face of the unexpected. Leaders should put themselves in the same category as athletes and pilots; they need to have the strength to endure and reach their destination. If you don't want to give up, start with not giving up on yourself. Give yourself a break when you know you need one.

RESOLUTION RUBS OFF ON OTHERS

When leaders demonstrate resolution, the staff develops the confidence to believe that their efforts can culminate in real achievement. Taking their cues from a resolute leader, they will persevere to reach the end goal. When challenges seem insurmountable and fatigue and hopelessness begin to creep in, a leader with a fierce sense of determination and a steadfast will to succeed can rally a team to carry on and complete the mission. Resolution is the ability to sustain the vision of what is possible, while dealing with and rising above adversity, and staying focused until the task is completed.

The resolved leader knows there has got to be a way to figure it out. Leaders will encounter challenges that will test their willpower and their commitment. We can be distracted and dart from one issue to another, never getting anywhere, but nothing great will ever happen that way. All big endeavors are tests of our resolve. The bigger the goal, the harder it is to see the finish line and the more resolution is needed to get there.

When we finish what we start, we motivate others to do the same.

TAKING WING

The hallmark of a winner is her staying power, her stick-to-itiveness. We don't usually read about the time, the patience, the commitment, effort, doubt, failure, despair, and tribulation that individuals and organizations go through on their paths to greatness.

In 1903, Orville and Wilbur Wright changed history. On that day, Orville was the first person to fly a heavier-than-air, powered airplane. The *Wright Flyer* flew a distance of 120 feet at an average speed of 6.8

miles per hour for a total of twelve seconds. Take two deep breaths. Likely twelve seconds just passed. In that same amount of time, two brothers solved the mystery of flight. Sixty-six years later, Neil Armstrong walked on the moon. Twelve short seconds, only a few feet above the ground, skimming across the sands of Kitty Hawk, two resolute brothers opened the door to modern aviation.

What did it take to fly for twelve seconds? Years of failure and disappointment. Long trips from Dayton, Ohio, in a boat of questionable seaworthiness over the Albemarle Sound to the desolate spit of the Outer Banks. Loneliness and isolation. Blowing sand and chilling winds. Limited resources and physical exhaustion. No one paid them for their time and efforts; they had no grants or venture capitalists knocking on their doors. From their first attempts in 1899 to their successful flight four years later, the Wright brothers made over a thousand attempts, working through the hopelessness, the unpredictable weather, and the elusive specter of success on the remote dunes of Kitty Hawk.

What was it about these two brothers that enabled them to accomplish what so many before them had failed to achieve? It has been said that probably the single most important motivator in the Wrights' program was their resolution. In a letter written on May 13, 1899, to Octave Chanute, a respected leader in the emerging field of aeronautics, Wilbur Wright wrote, "For some years I have been afflicted with the belief that flight is possible to man. My disease has increased in severity and I feel that it will soon cost me an increased amount of money if not my life." Today their achievement is etched in granite, high atop sand-swept dunes, reminding millions of visitors that their flight was "Achieved by dauntless resolution."

Looking back over my own career, I recognize that my most challenging times were the times where my resolve was tested the most. It has been in the face of repeated setbacks and opposition that I have learned to buck up, dig in my heels, and keep going.

One of those times was when I made a commitment to establish commercial air service for my community. I soon realized that I had picked an exceedingly difficult field to master. Financially volatile, strangled with red tape, highly regulated, and unrelentingly risky—that's the world of commercial passenger air service. My entry into this world, however, taught me some powerful and invaluable lessons, not least of which was a whole new grasp of the meaning of resolution, which made taking a toothbrush to the shower tiles start to look like child's work.

■

A THANKS TO THE AIRPORT AUTHORITY

As the sun set over the Albemarle Sound on November 23, 1996, I was putting the final touches on a presentation I was to make that evening to the Dare County Airport Authority. When I left the tiny two-room office that served as headquarters for our airline venture, I was encouraged by laughter, claps on the shoulder, and expressions of "Go get 'em!" and "Good luck!" With a lot of confidence and a healthy dose of rattled nerves, I tucked a flipchart under my arm and briskly walked across the parking lot at Dare County Regional Airport in Manteo, North Carolina. I was on that night's agenda to present the business plan for my new start-up—SouthEast Air.

The idea for the venture had started when I was a taking flight lessons at Dare County Regional. At the time I was CEO of B&B on the Beach, a leading vacation management company. I was intimately aware of the need for safe and reliable air transportation for the 10 million visitors who came to the Outer Banks each year. As I spent more time at the airport and got more familiar with the industry, the wheels of my mind began turning. With a background in marketing and a passion for the skies, I decided to step up to the edge and jump into the world of air transportation.

The Dare County Airport Authority had been trying to establish air service to the Outer Banks for decades and had recently spent $30,000 on the development and preparation of a report by an aviation consulting group. The report demonstrated the need and demand for air service to our burgeoning tourist mecca. After conducting many interviews with different airlines across the country, the authority had high hopes that an established and recognized airline would decide to initiate service on the Outer Banks.

The nine-member authority was made up of retired Navy, Army, and Air Force pilots, many in their seventies, several of whom had flown in World War II. There were no women on the board. In their day, women weren't allowed to fly in combat. It had only been three years (1994) since Lieutenant Kara Hultgreen became the first woman allowed to fly combat in the Navy.

On that November evening, mine was the airline lured to the challenge of introducing commercial air service to the Outer Banks. SouthEast Air was a new start-up headed by me, a feisty woman armed with an MBA and a commercial pilot rating, as well as a lot of years of experience in the Outer Banks tourist market. I presented my strategic plan. I asked for the authority's support, requesting that we be partners and work together for success. The authority controlled the rent, the fuel prices, and all leased space, airport operations and management, navigational facilities, runways, and hangars. In other words, they had a stranglehold on the biggest line items in the budget for any airline, as well as the facilities and operational equipment necessary for carrying out commercial flights. I needed their support and cooperation.

Today when I look back on that meeting, I realize that from the moment I stepped up to the podium with my flipchart, most of the board members had already decided that no way in hell was a woman going to head up this project. Yet despite resistance, documents were signed granting me the legal authority to start operations. On the surface it looked like I had a green light. But behind the signatures were as-yet-unexpressed intentions of key individuals to make my chances of success very, very difficult. Their signatures said "Go," but their attitudes and expectations said, "Not in my lifetime." My path forward would be filled with disagreement, obstruction, negativity, and a lack of support.

The demand for convenient, professional, reliable air service proved to be strong. Within six months, we had expanded our fleet from one small plane to three aircraft, including a five-passenger, twin-engine Cessna. We hired two more professional pilots and recruited a full-time aviation mechanic. Our reservation board was completely full. Yet it seemed that the more successful we were, the less cooperative the airport management became, and the more determined they were to undermine our efforts. We found ourselves constantly dealing with obstacles that were overtly or covertly thrown in our path.

Our requests for a fuel quantity discount went unanswered for over a year. While the freewheeling air tour operators enjoyed steep discounts and unlimited use of the terminal as a pickup point, we were denied access to the lovely, well-designed, state-provided terminal. They closed the main runway for scheduled repairs in July and August, the busiest time of year for us—a decision that was made without consulting us. That closure cost us hundreds of flights and tens of thousands of dollars in revenues. It was an expensive and time-consuming inconvenience to not be able to depend on our home base during high season.

But in the midst of constant curveballs, roadblocks, and disruptions from airport operations and the authority, I remained resolute in the goal of establishing commercial air service for the Outer Banks. Our motto was: "If we can't do it, it can't be done."

In 1997, we partnered with Cape Air out of Barnstable, Massachusetts, to add regularly scheduled service to our charter operations. Cape Air provided (and continues to provide) safe, efficient, and reliable air service to the seasonal tourist markets of Cape Cod, Nantucket, and Martha's Vineyard. Cape Air had the appropriate aircraft for Dare County's airstrip and a great reputation, and they were in expansion mode. I worked with them and their staff to coordinate the complex events and actions required to get scheduled service off the ground.

On April 2, 1998, Cape Air flew the first scheduled flight from the Outer Banks to Norfolk, Virginia. Finally, after many years of effort, the Outer Banks had professional, reliable, and regularly scheduled air service.

My resolution was constantly tested during those years. There were nights when I returned home fatigued and in utter despair. I spent countless hours with my attorney, who kept me focused and professional. My commitment to my community, my team, and our passengers fueled and supported my resolve to succeed. The lessons I learned from that venture could fill another book. But one of the greatest is resolution, the strength to persevere despite obstacles, to keep trying in the face of adversity, and to finish what I started.

Today, when I face any challenge, be it big or small, personal or business, simple or chaotic, I can thank the cantankerous old men on that conservative authority. They unintentionally solidified my determination and strengthened my resolve.

Resolve is reinforced by clarity of purpose, sticking to the plan, and hard work. Leaders are like top athletes: they are expected to win races, to have the strength to keep running when others quit. Take care of yourself, stay strong mentally and emotionally, and always finish what you start.

RESOLUTION

The following exercise will help you resolve a project or goal that has eluded your attempts to successfully complete.

I. Identify a situation that you find challenging, tiresome, relentless, and frustrating. (For example: an important relationship, a new product line, a major acquisition, or a specific project or sales target.) Describe the situation.

_____

_____

_____

_____

II. Answer the following questions as they relate to the situation:

1. Is a definitive solution or closure really important? *If not, go back and identify a different situation.*

2. Are you tired of trying to resolve the situation?

3. Do you find yourself becoming impatient when addressing it?

4. Have you thought of giving up on finding solutions?

5. Do you feel you are unfit, physically or mentally, to solve the problem?

If you answered yes to any of these questions, you need an opportunity to stop thinking this issue to death. Do something to recharge your batteries and regain a positive attitude. Get away from work for a few days if you can, or if time is an issue, just take a walk or find a place to be alone and meditate. Give your brain a rest. When you feel like you are ready to attack the problem again, go on to the next step.

III. When you are completely overwhelmed and frustrated with a problem, it helps to go back to the purpose and passion that fueled you in the beginning. Write down the reasons for your underlying commitment to this situation, and what its resolution means to you.

_____

_____

_____

IV. To fulfill your commitments and accomplish your goals, you need structure. For the situation you have described, provide answers to the following:

    1. To resolve this, I need the following resources: _____

        _____

    2. To resolve this, I need involvement/support from the following people: _____

        _____

    3. My target date for reaching a resolution is: _____

    4. I will know I have been successful when: _____

        _____

V. When times are tough and your will is challenged, having someone else hold you accountable can help you reach the finish line. Share this situation with a trusted person and ask him or her to hold you to your goals for resolution.

VI. Don't forget to reward yourself for a job well done! When the issue is resolved, how will you celebrate the success?

_____

_____

4

FAITH

My view of our planet was a glimpse of divinity.

—Dr. Edgar D. Mitchell (b. 1930),
NASA astronaut, *Apollo 14*

I imagine that there is nothing quite like a view of the earth from outer space to remind us of how small we are in the grand scheme of the universe. I try to capture that feeling on dark starlit nights, allowing my imagination to wander as I gaze at the sky, watching for shooting stars and tracing the path of the Milky Way.

Yet despite rational acknowledgment of our relatively small stature in a world that ranges from atoms and quarks to the unimaginable voids of black holes, we continually get stuck thinking we have all the answers. The fact is we don't; I don't, you don't, they don't. The pope, rabbis, mullahs, CEOs, and presidents—all will come face to face with circumstances to which they have no answer, problems that defy the mightiest might and the strongest will. The fact is, we live and work in an uncertain world where everything can change in an instant. What we think is normal can rapidly spiral out of control. Earthquakes, floods, disease, death, accidents, terrorism, financial collapse . . . these and other occurrences can blindside us, leaving us with an uncomfortable feeling of helplessness, a sense of futility in the face of an uncertain future.

Such is the nature of life. As much as we want to control and plan, the world will continue to surprise us, and situations will arise in which we have no idea where to turn or what path to follow.

As a leader, this certainty of an uncertain future presents unique challenges. You are expected to stand tall at the helm and call the shots, no matter what you are facing. Your followers want you to be in control, or at least *seem* to be. People look to you to make sense of chaos, to impose order on mayhem, and to make the illogical seem logical. Yet despite your best attempts to stay in control, there will always be chaos, change, and randomness.

So where do leaders turn when they run out of answers? Where do you find comfort when key personnel defect and join the competition? How do you keep going when sickness pulls you down or an accident incapacitates you? Where is the comfort when economics dictates that you downsize, compromising the quality of individual lives? How do you hold on when trust is broken, when stalemates seem permanent, when the opposition gets the upper hand? What resources do you have when the rule books don't work and your strategies and options are used up? What do you do in the face of failure and defeat? Where do you turn?

WHAT IS FAITH?

I am going to share with you my version of faith, my experience of the role faith has played in my life, and some of my observations about how faith applies to leadership. The understanding and practice of faith is, of course, personal and unique. I am not attempting to tell you what faith should mean to you personally, how to express it or practice it, or how to specifically integrate it into your leadership. This is only my understanding of how it can fortify and strengthen your leadership conduct and your character.

For me, faith boils down to a belief that there is a grand scheme to the events of our lives beyond our ability or need to understand or control. Faith is a willingness to acknowledge that things happen for a reason. Faith supports an acceptance of reality for what it is. It allows the faithful to move beyond judgment, blame, and self-pity to look for what's needed now and what can be learned later. Faith is a belief that there is an unseen force that guides the universe and all things, the belief that we are not the be all and end all of life, that there is something greater than our own will at work. Faith is a belief that there is a wider field of knowledge, grace, and guidance that is accessible through humility, gratitude, and belief. Faith reminds me that when I do my best and try my hardest but things still don't go the way I expected, there is a reason; something better or different needs to occur. Faith lifts me above despair and opens my eyes to hope.

Most leaders develop strategies and goals to reach desired outcomes, and most leaders have had the agonizing experience of seeing their best-laid plans derailed. It is in those derailments, those failures and setbacks, that the role of faith distinguishes those who succumb to despair from those who have the faith to rise above it. With faith, you know that there is something greater at work, something more to learn, some reason for the unwanted outcome that has not yet revealed itself. With faith a leader knows that when an unseen hand applies an emergency brake to an endeavor, it is on your behalf and for your benefit.

BLACK MONDAY

In 1987 there was a stock market crash called Black Monday. Along with the stock market, the second-home real estate market also collapsed. At the time I was in year three of a start-up in, you guessed it, the second-home real estate market. When I initially entered the real estate business in 1984, the vacation areas of Duck and Corolla, North Carolina, were just being discovered. Demand was high and business was very good. That was until tax laws were changed in 1987 eliminating the benefit of deducting losses on an investment home directly from bottom-line income on personal tax returns. That tax treatment had been a real boon to my start-up, and its removal coupled with the stock market collapse put the brakes on sales and momentum. In the next six months, my company's gross income was cut in half. All the profits generated from three long years of hard work seemed to vanish. It was frightening and depressing. Using my business know-how, I readjusted budgets, maintained communication with staff and customers, and hunkered down to wait until things turned around—whenever that would be. I no doubt appeared strong and in command to others, but I was physically and emotionally exhausted and on the verge of giving up.

I knew that I needed to get away, that I was being sucked into a numbing world of despair and hopelessness. So I retreated to a cousin's condo at a ski resort in Virginia and sat in front of a TV set for three days. In between crying and sleeping I channel-surfed.

At the time I was more or less faithless, or at least was not cognizant of faith as an important value in my leadership. But on day three of my zombie retreat, a TV evangelist popped up on a random channel talking about hope, and he caught my attention. I started to think about hope: what exactly it was, why it had left me and where it had gone. Most important, how could I get it back?

And then miraculously, hope just reentered my mind. I got excited about going back to my company and tackling the challenges at hand, creating new strategies and redefining the financials and making it all work. Just when I needed it, hope appeared. At the time, I was just relieved to be rid of the anxiety. But today, with faith, my hopelessness would have been minimized by the assurance that answers would be forthcoming.

Hope is a key ingredient of faith. It would be several years before I acknowledged the role of faith, as you will see later in this chapter. But I believe that faith was there in 1987, that faith is always there, ready to lend a hand, if you are receptive to it.

START BY BELIEVING

Faith can knock on your door, but the question is, will you recognize it? Sometimes you get a sign and luck out. But to really consistently understand and practice the value and strength of faith, you have to believe. Without faith, the incessant challenges of life can wear you down and extinguish hope. With faith, you can rise above uncertainty and ward off despair. Faith can provide reassurance that we live in a world of immense resources, a world of infinite ideas and unimaginable solutions. Faith can offer you assurance that there is a way out, that there is truth in the reality you're facing. But you have to believe.

Believe that there is a force greater than yourself, a benevolent power that generates love, hope, beauty, and a world of unseen but actualized miracles. *Believe* that there are forces at work in your life and leadership far greater than your limited human capacities. *Believe* that there is a purpose for every life and a reason for whatever reality confronts you. *Believe* that, although you can't see it, faith is immeasurable. *Believe* that when you do what you know is right, you've done your best, even if the ultimate purpose and consequence may not be revealed immediately, or even in your lifetime.

Belief is where an understanding of faith begins. Experienced leaders know that at some point they will encounter situations that defy logic, problems too big for the brightest team, and forces that are totally out of their control. With faith, you can believe that when you have done all you can, life will deal its hand, and all things shall pass.

A FLUFFY VALUE IN A WORLD OF FACTS

Business is a science, a well-designed blueprint, a structure that when applied to a project or endeavor seeks to make sense, create balance, and organize activities for maximum performance. Business is a very left-brain activity: no-nonsense, important, significant, intellectual, rational, and willful. In our businesses we want concrete answers.

On the other hand, faith is immeasurable and invisible. Faith is an intangible, abstract concept. It can't be measured or quantified. It can't be incorporated into an annual report or a critical presentation. It is seldom, if ever, mentioned in business plans or tacked on to the introduction of significant bills in Congress. Faith is largely absent from the curriculum of MBA programs. The business models and institutional behaviors that have developed over the past few decades leave little room for ambiguity, abstraction, or nuance. Consequently, faith is a rare topic in leadership.

But faith introduces patience into a world of instant gratification and short-term results. In the face of criticism and controversy, faith provides a calm and steady hand. Faith elevates perspectives beyond self-serving interests. With faith, a leader can help others to achieve their potential. Faith allows a leader to replace despair and doubt with hope. Without faith, leaders can succumb to self-pity, despair, and resignation. In the face of defeat, many leaders break down physically and emotionally. Faith is the lift that leaders need as they face opposing winds. Faith can elevate potential to reality and lift the veil of helplessness. It offers the wisdom of patience, the quiet strength of a calm and steady hand.

PATIENCE

Faith demands patience, and the understanding that we cannot always be in control of all the outcomes of our decisions. Sometimes it takes decades to see the rewards of your efforts; sometimes you don't see the rewards in your lifetime. When I announced that my real estate company was going public, many of the managers left to start competing firms. These were not just important management personnel; they were friends, almost like brothers and sisters. We had grown the company together, had celebrated our successes and comforted each other in our failures and disappointments. For them to jump ship, and to work against us instead of for us, was an unexpected and crushing blow. As for me, with the sale of my company and a myriad of unexpected consequences that came with it, I had little idea of how my own life was going to proceed, or what my career might look like in a year, much less in a decade or two. The future seemed lonely and scary. I was frightened by the prospect of change and the uncertainties that lay ahead.

However, holding on to the belief that with faith all things happen for a reason, I did my best to shy away from judgment and fear and continued to forge ahead, focusing on the many decisions that were facing me professionally and personally. Eventually, the reasons for those defections and other heart-wrenching events that occurred during that transition revealed themselves. Ten years later, personal lives and fortunes had been redefined in ways that no one could have predicted. Today there are prosperous and dynamic companies that would not exist if my friends and coworkers had not had the courage to go out on their own. My own life has found its rhythm and purpose in leadership speaking and writing, endeavors that might not have happened without the difficult transitions around the public offering and their related consequences.

Today I can see that most things in my life have had a purpose far beyond my understanding at the time. With faith, I believe that my life and career, my very purpose for being, is composed of all of the events and relationships of my life; everything, the good and the bad, has helped make me the person that I am, a work in progress constantly being sculpted and perfected.

A CALM AND STEADY HAND

How easy it is to fall victim to stress, anxiety, and worry. I remember heading out to an important business meeting a few years back and how noisy my internal critic was; my head was filled with anxious and negative thoughts. I was worrying about all of the variables I knew I would not be able to control, and focusing on all the things that could go wrong. I was weighted down with nonconstructive self-doubt and anxiety, rather than calmly considering rational alternatives to the problems I was facing.

Walking hurriedly down a crowded New York City sidewalk, I happened to notice a magnificent cathedral. Impulsively, I decided to duck in to seek a moment of quiet away from the noise and frenzy of the streets. Once inside, I was drawn to a very small chapel containing only two chairs. In the front of the tiny alcove sat a man with his back to me, hunched over with his head in his hands. In an impeccable suit, Bluetooth on, and looking every bit the important businessman, he was quietly sobbing. Behind him was a winged angel, six feet tall, kneeling, with her arms outstretched and hair cascading down her marble back. The angel seemed to be supporting and soothing the businessman. Did he feel a spiritual presence? Did he find respite and grace in that moment? I can't answer for him, but I did. That marble angel reminded me to let go of my worries. She gave me a fresh and a renewed perspective. My concerns were not worth dwelling on.

I left the cathedral and reentered the hustle and bustle of the city streets, but I was different. I was calm. I knew without a shadow of doubt that all was well, that I was prepared for the meeting, and that, with an invisible hand on my shoulder guiding me, what needed to happen would happen. Faith had replaced my ego-driven worries.

I hailed a cab and was swept downtown. When I arrived at my destination, my anxiety had been replaced with a sharpened awareness of my surroundings: the people, the architecture, the unfamiliar environment. I was filled with a calm assurance of my aptitude and an appreciation of the opportunity awaiting me. I knew that I had done my best to prepare, that I was fully present, and I called upon my faith to bring out the best in me.

My presentation went as smooth as silk; I was hardly aware of myself or my words, but they flowed. The outcome was positive, partnerships were initiated, and new pathways and projects came into being. A brief moment of grace from a random decision to enter a cathedral allowed my human-driven worry to be replaced by a calm confidence borne on the wings of faith.

FRAMING WORK IN FAITH

When you lead with a belief in serving others through your product or service, you provide the gift of purpose to your organization and its people. Acknowledging that work has meaning beyond production, efficiency, and profits is a powerful motivator. We all need to be reminded of our potential to make a difference. When you frame work in the context of sustainability and contribution, perspectives are elevated from the mundane to the meaningful. Prayer, recognition, meditation, or even just a moment of silence are all ways to see ourselves as part of something much more expansive.

As part of a consulting project, I once attended a board meeting of a successful public utility. The board chair asked one of the members if he would open the meeting with a prayer. In this room filled with strong and independent men and women, the chair placed the event within the context of faith. He acknowledged the board's responsibility to the greater good of the community and the employees, and he pointed out the limitations of being human and asked for insight and guidance from a source more infinite and loving than we as individuals could imagine. This prayer was not memorized. It wasn't from a religious text. It came straight from this man's heart. "We are here to serve," he said, "to bring out the best in ourselves in our commitment to contribute to others." That brief prayer put the meeting into a larger context and brought the group together in gratitude, humility, and purpose.

THE POWER OF FAITH IN OTHERS

One of the most powerful motivational statements a leader can make is, "I have faith in you." So many workers long to hear those words. There are probably people in your life right now who would walk a million miles just to hear that from you.

Faith from a leader can motivate and inspire others in unimaginable ways. When a leader, parent, or mentor states a belief in another's ability to overcome adversity and to do the right thing, it can be the key to that person's success.

I begin one of my leadership courses with an exercise that asks attendees to identify the leader who has inspired them the most. I explain that it can be a famous leader, present or historical; it can be a political figure, a church leader, a past or current boss, even a relative. I give them time to consider and reflect on who in their life has exerted the most positive influence on the development of their leadership character. When the time comes to stand up and share, most recount emotional stories of people who took the time to help them along the way, ordinary people who believed in them. Rarely does anyone cite famous leaders as having a lot of influence; it is almost always the everyday people who take the time to grace our lives when we are in need.

When I reflect on my career and development as a leader, I am grateful for the many people who had faith in me: my mother; my seventh-grade teacher Dr. McClung; Lee Tate, the CEO of C&P Telephone in Richmond, Virginia; Bill Patterson, a successful businessman and entrepreneur in my hometown; brave friends who flew with me when I was a beginner; clients who trusted me with their business well before my success was assured. I would not be where I am today without the faith of those who took the time to tell me they had faith that I could do it.

The power of faith also extends to teams and organizations. If you have someone working for you, or a team hard at work on a compelling challenge, the expression of your heartfelt faith in and support of their ability to succeed can have a great effect on the outcome. You can't hide disdain or disbelief in others; they will pick up on it and suffer under the weight of negative expectation. Believing in another elevates potential into reality.

BEYOND DESPAIR AND DOUBT

How quickly despair and doubt can take over a battered leader's attitude! But these emotions have no place in leadership. When you find yourself slipping into despair, step away from the cause. Find a quiet place to pray or meditate, take a walk or a swim, or listen to soothing music; do your best to empty your head of despairing thoughts. Try to regain your faith in the future, even if you don't know the outcome and things are looking bleak. When a leader loses faith—whether in a person, the outcome of a project, or an important negotiation—it's time to find a way to regain it or cut your involvement. People and projects suffer terribly under the direction of someone who doesn't believe in them.

WHY FAITH IS IN SHORT SUPPLY IN LEADERSHIP

If faith is such a great thing, why don't all leaders possess and use it? And if faith is such an important attribute, why is it often taboo to talk about it in a business setting? Why is faith often rejected and excluded from our leadership conversations and practices?

Status quo for business is that what you see is what you get—tightly crafted and measured performance expectations, short-term strategies to ensure short-term results, metrics, ratios, spreadsheets. These leadership tools are important, but they won't address the challenges that go beyond our human understanding. Often what you fail to see or believe in, you won't get. That is where faith resides—in the unseen. Consequently, faith is largely unrecognized and underutilized in a profession largely dominated by logic.

Another reason faith is largely missing in our leadership conduct is its relationship to the concept of control. When leaders insist on the appearance of being in control and on a black-and-white interpretation of reality, they are denying the ambiguous nature of our world. When leaders hide their weaknesses, obscure difficult truths, refuse to acknowledge their limitations, and strive to show that they are invincible, they are bucking a universal truth: as humans, we are all flawed. Every individual, every group or organization, every endeavor has weaknesses and stress points and cracks. To deny this is to deny what it means to be human. Even the best leaders in the world are vulnerable to disappointment and missteps. What differentiates the truly great from the rest of the pack is humility and faith in the face of any setback.

Yet another reason faith is met with skepticism in the halls of business, politics, and government is the widespread use of faith as a cover-up for unethical and immoral behavior. Thanks to the highly publicized hypocritical actions of so many religious leaders and politicians who spent careers behind the false mask of religious faith, faith is often equated with deceit. In recent years, we have learned of the hypocritical choices of many formerly respected and revered politicians; John Edwards and Mark Sanford are just two examples. Righteousness is often a cover-up for unethical behavior, as was the case with Jim and Tammy Bakker, Jimmy Swaggart, Ted Haggard, and Vaughan Reeves. There are leaders in all fields and at all levels who righteously profess their faithfulness, only to be later revealed as dishonest, unethical, and sometimes criminal.

Faith has also come to be regarded as a solution for the weak, a cop-out. It has been corrupted and distorted by greed and self-serving interests. Heads of state, kings and queens, community organizers, and preachers too often inappropriately use the concept of faith to cajole others to follow them into dangerous and unethical territory. Misinterpretation of faith is at the heart of terrorism, which poses one of the world's greatest threats.

It's easy to understand why faith in leadership is a skirted issue. But don't let the poor examples of a few deter you from adding the power of faith to your leadership arsenal.

FINDING FAITH

Faith is a gift, and like any gift you need to be able to receive it. Start by being open to the concept of faith and looking for it—in the random acts of kindness that occur in your world, in a positive outcome from defeat, in an unexpected turn of events. Start by seeking, asking, and being receptive. You need to be willing to believe that faith exists. This belief can begin with a simple prayer of gratitude for what you do have and a request to know and live in faith. Take a minute or two out of your day to open yourself to receiving faith in your own unique way. There are many avenues to faith; the first step is to ask for it.

Where else can leaders find faith? Maybe in an unexpected hug or pat on the back. Perhaps when walking through a quiet forest or stopping long enough to take in an incredible sunset. Faith can be found in a moment of silence before a critical conversation or a contentious board meeting. Some seek faith in religious settings and buildings; others find it in nature. Faith can find you in the words of a poem or a prayer. Faith can show up in an unexpected phone call from an old friend or an act of kindness by a coworker. Faith can often be accessed by simply closing your door, taking a few deep breaths, and asking for guidance.

Evidence of faith is all around you. It can appear at the most random moments. When faith shows up, savor it. Here is a story of how faith found me; without it, I doubt I'd be writing this book.

SIDE ROADS, SHALE, AND THE TWENTY-THIRD PSALM

In 1998, my ex-husband (whom I will call Tim) and I were approached by one of our clients about the possibility of our resort business going public. This individual had a successful track record for venture capital investments and public offerings. He and two other partners had the idea that the sun, ski, and sand resorts that had been an important part of their own family vacations were fertile ground for a relatively new concept called a "rollup." Tim and I met with our friend over dinner and discussed the possibilities. We had always maintained that we would one day sell the company and move on to other ventures, but we were currently entertaining the idea of offering it to the employees. After long discussions, we decided that being part of the rollup would satisfy our desire to sell yet maintain the integrity of the company, the management structure, and the beliefs and ideals of the organization. The new entity would be called ResortQuest International.

When we announced the news to our employees, I remember one of the venture partners telling a gathering of our employees that nothing would change. I naïvely believed him.

We went public in 1998. One of the first decisions made by the public entity that now owned the property was to centralize and standardize. They would merge twelve homegrown entities into an efficient, streamlined, profitable, and saleable national brand, benefiting from what they assumed would be shared operational efficiencies and economies of scale. The effort to homogenize, however, would prove to be no easy task. These different vacation management firms were located in some of the most beautiful and remote places in the country: Maui, Vail, Nantucket, the Outer Banks. Most had been created and headed up by feisty entrepreneurs in the 1970s and '80s who were equipped with small amounts of start-up capital, copious spunk and stamina, and high levels of independence and eccentricity.

Aspen, Colorado, was chosen for ResortQuest's first foray into centralizing this collection of entrepreneurs and their equally spirited staff members. They held a company-wide training session to bring all of the different companies' software programs into one central and standardized reservation and operational system. But the leadership hadn't counted on the strong resistance of the people responsible for the different resorts' individual IT systems. When these individuals had been hired to put reservation and accounting systems in place, there were no tech geeks around, no Best Buys, no troubleshooters, and no prepackaged software options for this specialized cottage industry. Most of the companies had contracted with trusted IT individuals in their regions and developed software that addressed their specific needs and allowed for a lot of customized input, change, and flexibility as the companies grew. These custom-designed reservation systems fit each company perfectly, and no one was very happy about overhauling everything into a new, less-personalized system. The customized accounting systems met the diverse legal and fiduciary needs of state realty laws and guidelines. They had been vital support structures in the growth and development of these vacation companies that started as small mom-and-pops and grew into multimillion-dollar providers of outstanding customer service for vacationers.

I arrived in Aspen a day later than the rest, and I was looking forward to joining Tim and my colleagues. I'd gotten an earlier flight than expected, and although I arrived early, my luggage didn't. When I saw Tim in the terminal, I sensed a great deal of tension and anxiety. I asked him what was wrong, and he said that there was a lot of bickering and discord occurring among our staff members. I suggested we take a drive together to catch up, unwind, and kill a little time before the next flight arrived with my luggage.

So we went on a short drive in the Aspen countryside. We couldn't see much in those early evening hours except the outline of mountains and the large shadows of clumps of trees. After a few miles, Tim pulled onto the side of the road, turned off the car, and said quite matter-of-factly, "I have something for you." He handed me a small gift-wrapped box. Surprised, I unwrapped it and opened a velveteen box containing a pair of diamond earrings. Stunned, I looked at him with questioning eyes. He simply said, "I've always wanted you to have these." I put them on, thanked him, and that was that. He started the car and we headed back to the airport.

After retrieving my slowpoke luggage, we caught up with our team from North Carolina. There was a lot of anxiety and unhappiness on the part of several of our key staff members; there were tears and blame and frustration, some directed at the new corporate entity and some directed at Tim, who had replaced me as CEO the previous year, allowing me to move into my aviation pursuits. As the night wore on, conversations became even more heated; eventually, the discussions became unreasonable and pointless. By the time Tim and I returned to our condo, I was exhausted.

The next morning, everyone headed to IT training, but as the retired CEO, it wasn't necessary for me to attend. Curious and a little confused by the previous night's earring episode, I decided to return to the spot on the road where Tim had given them to me. My head and heart were filled with worry, confusion, and an impending sense of loss. The weight of the changes Tim and I had been through with our company was heavy. I was also in the throes of selling my small airline—a venture I had undertaken with more intellectual, physical, emotional, and financial investment than anything I had done before. If I thought about it much (which I didn't want to do), I could have easily come to the conclusion that the world I was accustomed to might be falling apart around me.

It wasn't difficult to retrace the previous night's short drive from the airport down a country road to a small gravel pull off. As I walked away from the car I came upon a little roadside Buddhist garden dedicated to the memory of someone's wife; it felt like a special place. In the distance, large stands of aspens and groves of spruce pine stood lazily in the morning sun. I climbed over the fence and looked with awe at nature's spectacular tableau in front of me. I was so moved, I lay down in the wildflowers and let the sun ease my worry and confusion. Soon, my anxieties began to drift away.

When I stood up, my attention was drawn to a small mountain that beckoned me, and I began climbing the steep incline. Halfway up I hit a shale face. As I continued, my feet kept slipping and the shale slipped with me. I realized that if I fell, it would be a long way down and that I would probably break a few things. Furthermore, my landing spot would be in a deserted field away from the road, making it unlikely that anyone would find me anytime soon. Calculating the risk, I carefully made my way horizontally off the shale face onto a more hospitable side of the mountain and continued my ascent. With a sense of leaving my worries below me, I reached the summit. Turning in a circle, I was bathed in warm sunlight and surrounded by brilliant blue skies and an unbelievably beautiful vista of trees, flowers, and mountains. I was overwhelmed by powerful feelings of sadness, joy, awe, wonder, and gratitude. I felt strong and sturdy, yet weak and overwhelmed at the same time. It was a magnificent experience. As Hilary Cooper said, "Life is not measured by the number of breaths we take, but by the moments that take our breath away." This was a definite "take my breath away" moment.

As if something were compelling me, I began to recite the Twenty-third Psalm, a verse from the Bible that I had repeated by rote and with no sense of connection or meaning for most of my life. But that day, I recited it aloud, to the wind and the sky, and for the first time, the words meant something.

And for the first time in my life I knew that I was experiencing the presence of God.

Feeling humble, I cried. I thanked God for revealing Himself to me; after all these years of struggle, I now knew that all was well—faith had finally found me and would lighten the weight of the challenges I faced and the burdens that I was carrying. As I descended the mountain and retraced my steps through the field, over the fence, past the Buddhist garden, and back to the car, I was the same person I had been an hour before, yet I was completely transformed. I left that mountain with an additional pair of eyes—the eyes of the soul, offering a new perspective and a sense of wisdom, acceptance, and humility.

With one big sweep of grace, gone were anxieties and worries that I had accepted as normal for a hardworking CEO and driven entrepreneur. As I drove away from the sun, the shale, and the Twenty-third Psalm, I knew that life and leadership as I had known them were changing in ways I couldn't yet fathom. In the face of an uncertain and changing future, I now saw my world through a lens much wider than my rational view. Faith had found me and offered an elevated perspective that included a willingness to admit to not having all the answers—and being okay with that.

I headed back to town to rejoin my colleagues with more empathy and encouragement for their issues. I looked forward to my return to SouthEast Air, my most precious business endeavor, with an eye toward what would be required to dismantle it, sell off the equipment, find new positions for my staff, and outsource my clients. My feelings of dread were replaced by an eagerness for a new experience—taking something apart as opposed to my proven record as one who builds. I was open to the pathways and solutions that I knew would appear. Miraculously, within two months of that trip to Aspen, I met an individual who had recently undergone the long and arduous process of closing a family business that he had inherited from many generations of forebears. With empathy and experience, he guided and supported me, technically and emotionally, through the selling off, the laying off, the writing off, and the shutting down of SouthEast Air.

Although I was losing the comfort and familiarity of my real estate business and my airline, these losses formed the springboard for my path as a champion of great leadership in our society. These setbacks have been potent catalysts for my growth as an individual and as a leader. With faith, I knew these things to be true. With faith, I now know that setbacks were guideposts to growth.

Since that mountaintop experience in Aspen, I now observe my life within the context of a bigger picture. I consider it my responsibility to live my life to its fullest potential and to contribute my talents and resources to the fulfillment of a better world. Faith has proven to be the most interesting, diverse, intriguing, and reassuring tool that I have. It has enriched the strength of my leadership conduct far beyond what I learned in six years of graduate business study and thirty years of hands-on leadership experience, and has been far more helpful than the hundreds of business books I have read, the risks I have taken, the mergers, and the IPO (initial public offering).

I am no longer chained by worry and anxiety, or deterred by self-doubt or negative expectations or opinions. I continue to strive to do my best in all endeavors, to work hard, to identify and utilize the resources I need to accomplish goals, to achieve strategies, and to surmount obstacles. But I do so without attaching my ego to the outcome, without getting worked up when things don't go the way I expected. Aggravation has been replaced with patience, resentment has given way to tolerance and respect, and detours have become adventures. I believe that faith is the icing on the cake for any leader. It is the one attribute that can bring the heart to the forefront and light up a person from the inside out.

In the end, faith is an individual choice. The experience of it varies from person to person, from religion to religion, from practice to practice. But if you are lucky enough to have it, faith can guide and support you as you extend your personal gifts to others and contribute to the world around you.

FAITH

I. Where Do You Turn?

Circle all of the things that you resort to when you are burned out, stressed, or frustrated:

A	B
Spending money	Solitude
Drugs	Art
Affairs	Poetry
Sports	Counseling
Internet	Music
Medication	Engaging a personal/business coach
Partying	Reading
Alcohol	Helping others
TV	Meditating
Eating	Writing
Work	Nature (hike, garden, get in/on water)
Other (list):_____	Praying
	Attending a retreat
	Contributing to your community
	Random acts of kindness
	Loving others
	Spending time with family
	Other (list):_____

Column A lists diversionary, often harmful activities that help you ignore problems. Column B lists activities that offer you time and space to reflect and seek solutions to your challenges.

If your choices are primarily in Column A, you might be avoiding issues that you feel are out of your control, issues that could be supported with faith. Life's biggest challenges are best addressed with a clear heart, an open mind, and a willingness to let go of having the answers.

II. Who Has Faith in You?

Write down two people who have had a significant impact on your life by having faith in you. Beside each name, write down what they believe about you that is significant:

1. _____

2. _____

If it is possible to do, make a point to tell these people what a difference they have made in your life.

III. Whom Do You Have Faith In?

Write down two people you have mentored through a strong faith in their potential. Beside each name, write down why you believed in the person:

1. _____

2. _____

If it is possible to do, make a point to tell these people how much you believe the person.

IV. Who Would Benefit From Your Faith?

Name one person who would benefit from your having faith in them and letting them know it:

1. _____

Make a point to tell him or her, and encourage him or her with your support and faith.

V. Doorways to Faith

Gratitude

List three things/people that you are grateful for:

1. _____

2. _____

3. _____

Adversity and Failure

List two failures in your career:

1. _____

_____

2. _____

_____

Faith allows you to believe that all things happen for a reason. What did or can you learn from these failures?

1. _____

2. _____

VI. Faith Now and in the Future

Describe your current relationship to faith, and what you would like for it to be:

Currently, my faith is: _____

_____

I would like it to be:

_____

"With all of your science, can you tell me how it is, and when it is, that light comes into the soul?"

—HENRY DAVID THOREAU

3

INTEGRITY

Integrity is the foundation upon which other human values are built—trust, credibility, leadership—and that foundation can be damaged for a very long time, even irreparably, with the slightest crack in a person's or an organization's integrity.

—Michael D. Griffin (b. 1949),
NASA Administrator 2005–2009

When astronauts are launched into space, they are riding on a belief in the structural integrity of their spacecraft. They are also depending on the fundamental integrity of the men and women at NASA who are responsible for the many critical decisions affecting the safety and success of their mission. Just as seemingly small breaches of structural integrity—such as a broken O-ring or a rip in foam insulation—can jeopardize an entire mission and the lives of those on board, so too can small breaches of integrity jeopardize the ability of leaders to be effective, and even bring down powerful organizations.

What is this ingredient so fundamental to successful leadership?

Integrity is standing up for what you know to be right and true. It is sticking to what you believe, no matter what. Integrity is knowing who you are and what you believe in, and living and working accordingly. If you profess to be an honest person but withhold the truth for fear of its consequence, then you are not operating with integrity. If you say you are an honest person and stand up for the truth regardless of the consequence then you have integrity. Integrity is when what you say aligns with what you do . . . when you walk the talk, so to speak.

To embody integrity, you need to know what you stand for—your values. If you know what your guiding principles are and stand by them, then you are a leader with integrity. In this sense, integrity is the glue that holds your values together, defining the person that you are. It is your coat of armor, protecting and preserving who you are at your core and keeping you in one piece. When you deviate, your character is questioned. People can intuit a disconnect when you say one thing and do another. When your integrity is questioned, it creates dissonance and results in an erosion of trust. And when you can't be trusted, you can't lead.

NOT JUST A PRETTY WORD

"Integrity" is an easy word to throw around in business and political discussions but often a challenging and elusive principle to enact day-to-day. Integrity often demands courageous and challenging behavior because it means doing things the right way, not necessarily the easy way. It's a lot easier to *say* that you have integrity than it is to demonstrate it when you are facing uncertain or frightening consequences.

Integrity is easier said than done.

I have a friend who is a man of utmost integrity. He is absolutely trustworthy and much respected and admired by his colleagues, his clients, and even his competitors. Over the many years I have known him, professionally and personally, I have witnessed his integrity in action. When the organization he served was rocked by change, many jumped ship. Not him. He stayed. When times got tough and CEOs came and went—some good, some really bad—he stayed. When there was no leadership, he stayed, giving those around him some sense of security in a chaotic time of uncertainty. He was loyal to customers and the members of his team who stayed with him. And today, when so many have been knocked down by bad economic times, he is still standing, successful, supported by his customers, respected by his colleagues. His marriage of forty years is strong. He lives his beliefs. And one of those is loyalty. He is a man whom others believe in; they can count on him to be there, to be loyal to them and to his organization. For me, he exemplifies integrity.

Too many leaders compromise their integrity, especially in the face of losing their job, a promotion, or a raise. Leaders must hold themselves to higher standards than that.

Once I worked with an executive who talked the talk, but when push came to shove, he turned his back on his professed beliefs. Though he was the head of human resources, he ignored grievous abuses of power from a domineering and controlling CEO. What the staff observed was a disconnect between the person who was supposed to protect and serve them and his actual behavior, which seemed to disregard their interests. The executive had only a few years to go before reaching the golden parachute age for retirement with a full benefits package, and he wasn't going to rock the boat if it would jeopardize his financial well-being. This breach of integrity created cynicism and resentment throughout the company. It ripped a hole in the moral fiber of the organization.

It is incumbent on leaders to act with the highest integrity and to risk their needs for the good of the whole; this is a tenant of good leadership.

CAN YOU FACE THE CONSEQUENCES OF TRUTH?

When tested, are you willing and able to stand for what you believe in? Are you willing to do what's right, even at the risk of your own career security? Do you know what you value? Do you stand for the principles of your leadership and organization? Do you make decisions on behalf of your organization and its people, without regard to your own position and compensation?

These questions underlie the fundamental message of this book. As a leader, you must elevate your perspectives and operate with a deep respect for the profound influence you have on the lives of others. Do the right thing, be honest, put the interests of others before your own, and have the courage to embrace integrity regardless of the consequences. This is what *LiftOff Leadership* is all about.

WALKING THE TALK

Why is integrity so elusive in leadership? It is so important, yet we routinely overlook actions that lack integrity, choosing to say nothing. How can so many leaders and politicians say one thing and do another? Because we let them. Because too often we do the same thing ourselves. Even when we are talking the talk, we are not always walking the walk.

Most children are taught integrity: Keep your word. Honor your commitments. Do what you say you will. Tell the truth. Do the right thing. Surely we all heard these things growing up. As adults, we may read about integrity or hear the occasional lecture on the topic. Yet somewhere along the way the words get lost in translation. How many examples of failed integrity do we need to see in American business and politics before we understand that integrity is not just a word but is at the very core of our success as individuals, as leaders, as businesses, and as a society? How many Enrons, how many Madoffs, how many AIGs, and how many Mark Spencers do we need before we understand the need to insist on integrity as a core requirement for leadership?

The past decade has delivered some astonishing bankruptcies and dissolutions of once-revered companies. On November 10, 2008, Circuit City declared bankruptcy, and within a year there was nothing left. During the year preceding its dissolution, the CEO fired 3,400 of its tenured, loyal, experienced employees, replacing them with low-paid, inexperienced new hires. In the same year, that CEO received over $7 million in compensation and benefits. This self-serving act at a time of cutbacks and workforce reductions was a major breach of integrity, which delivered a crippling blow to the faltering foundations of a once-proud company.

Wachovia Bank was a respected household name in my upbringing in Virginia. It also collapsed due to breaches of integrity: deviating from a focus on the fundamental products and values of the company, implementing executive decisions to seek risky acquisitions, and putting the ambitions and desires of a select few ahead of the well-being of the organization. These glaring examples had headliner consequences and did immeasurable damage to thousands of investors, employees, and other constituents.

In organizations and businesses big and small, executives compromise themselves and others by not standing up for what they know is right. How many times have you sat in a meeting and not spoken up because you were afraid for your job? How often is the truth, so needed to create vibrant and sustainable companies, thwarted as people withhold information and lie to protect themselves? That is an ugly reality, but for leaders, it is not acceptable. Integrity is the only road to take.

I once sat in on a presentation by a vice president in charge of food services and listened to him laud the merits of a contract he had recently signed with a "green" waste-disposal firm. He held up the new contract as an example of his commitment to environmental efficiency. Several months later I had lunch in one of the employee cafeterias. I ate off of a nonrecyclable plastic plate and drank out of a nonbiodegradable plastic cup. The trash cans were overflowing with hundreds of single-use plastic utensils that were headed to everlasting life in a crowded landfill. It turned out that the vice president was saving money by not paying dishwashers. Where was the environmental accountability and stewardship he had preached? His choices were not in line with what he had claimed was important. Could I trust this executive?

I have coached many professionals whose morale and focus had fallen to dangerously low levels because feedback on their performance had not been forthcoming; feedback that a boss promised and repeatedly delayed or canceled. Every day CEOs say they will return calls and don't, say they care about leadership development and then cut the training budget, say they want transparency and then ask CFOs to "massage" the numbers for the next board meeting, and speak eloquently of fairness while simultaneously securing their own raise at a time of company-wide compensation cuts.

The thing about integrity is that once broken, it is often irreparable, no matter the scale of the breach. Little white lies, a lack of transparency, and small acts of dishonesty add up and break down the mortar of truth and honesty that hold together a giant corporation or a small community hospital. Cracks in critical areas will eventually erode the foundation to the point of collapse.

WHAT INTEGRITY LOOKS LIKE

Organizations with leaders at the helm who have integrity are the organizations where you can expect to have real, live, interested, and trained people on the customer-service line. These are the hospitals where physicians are encouraged to listen to and treat the total person. These are the political offices where constituents' voices are heard and respected. These are the politicians who know that judgment and condemnation are diversions from a collaborative, nonpartisan approach to solutions for the good of all. Endeavors that are defined by integrity foster creativity, discussion, and an openness to the possibility of failure (and trying again) in the pursuit of innovation. Companies led with integrity stay focused on their core principles and products, with a healthy dose of respect for their workforce and their customers. These companies can weather the tough times, the economic challenges, the demographic changes, and the stiff competition because employees trust and believe in their leaders, leaders who can be counted on to be true to their values and beliefs. Some positive examples are Timberland under Jeff Swartz, Costco under Jim Sinegal, Patagonia under Yvon Chouinard, and Southwest under Herb Kelleher.

Integrity isn't easy to measure. It's not a standard ratio on a financial statement. The best leaders know that the biggest asset they have is the quality, dedication, and productivity of the people who do the work to make things happen. If you lead with integrity and insist on the same in others, you will foster an environment of trust, loyalty, and collaboration, resulting in a group of people dedicated to doing their best to serve the needs of the organization.

A LACK OF INTEGRITY
IN LEADERSHIP = A HIGH PRICE TO PAY

As a leadership consultant, I often work with organizations that have become dysfunctional under the leadership of someone who lacks integrity. Even the smallest infractions have damaging results: a habitually late leader who requires others to be on time to meetings, a leader who insists on quick responses to her e-mails and phone calls but does not do the same in return, or a leader who preaches accountability to deadlines and repeatedly misses his own—all these erode trust and cause the company to suffer.

You might not think people are watching, but they are. You might not be aware of your own misaligned conduct. But give it some thought. What are your professed beliefs and foundational values? Are you a leader in healthcare but overweight and unhealthy due to stress? Are you a leader in banking but personally burdened with debt? These seemingly inconsequential, and often unconscious, infractions of integrity cause a slow decline in your credibility.

A leader who falls short on integrity will often retain power through emotional manipulation, short-term financial acumen, or diverting attention with the dazzle of his apparently superior business skills. But behind this smokescreen, the true impact of the leader will be a fearful, cynical, and resentful staff, who have lost trust in their leader, reverting instead to self-preservation, taking their cues from and protecting themselves against their leader's self-interest and hypocrisy. The needs of the larger organization, its community, and its constituents ultimately suffer as the vitality and goodness of the company drain away, sapped by the consistent breaches of integrity.

NO SHORTCUTS

In leadership, as in aviation, when you start taking self-serving shortcuts and do things that are out of line with the common good, you weaken your credibility and open fault lines that will ultimately threaten the stability of your organization.

Integrity is essential in aviation. From the structural integrity of an aircraft to the conduct of a pilot in adhering to FAA regulations, integrity is a critical component of safe flight. Integrity means doing the right thing. Integrity means that you don't bend and break rules for expediency.

To follow is a story that demonstrates potential consequences when a pilot decides to bend the rules and deviate from mandated, tightly designed directions for safe flight.

Let me start by giving you some context. When weather conditions obscure a pilot's ability to see the runway, he must adhere to "instrument approach plates," tightly engineered and drafted, FAA-approved dia-grams. They provide vertical and horizontal guidance for a safe approach to landing and touchdown, using cockpit navigational instruments. Pilots must model integrity in the actual conduct of flight, especially on instrument approaches where there is little room for error. When they break or bend the rules, they open the doors to uncertain and life-threat-ening consequences.

I can still hear my director of operations at SouthEast Air, a forty-year commercial pilot, telling me to never (and I mean *never*) deviate from the rules unless there was a stated and immediate emergency. He warned me that once I began to bend the rules, it would only get easier and easier to cut corners, and before I knew it, the stage would be set for disas-ter. He was a stickler for precision and tight, well-executed instrument approaches—with good reason.

■

THE NIGHT THE LIGHTS WENT OUT

On a foggy night in January 1997, my chief pilot and I decided to drive instead of fly. We were in Greenville, North Carolina, picking up an aircraft that had just undergone a required maintenance inspec-tion. We had checked with flight service and weather reports, so we knew that conditions throughout the northeastern part of the state were steadily deteriorating. By the time we were ready to fly home, the weather at our home base of Manteo, North Carolina, was well below the minimums required for safe landing. Heeding the warnings, we made the "no go" decision and rented a car and headed out on the lonely stretch of road across the sparsely populated northeast-ern part of the state. Within the next hour, the fog got thicker and visibility dropped. It was one of those nights when you could barely see your hand in front of your face. At a certain point, we remarked on how very dark it was outside. Then we realized why: there were no lights at all; no gas stations signs, no streetlights, no house lights. A power outage? Strange. The weather was soupy, but not stormy.

At about the same time we had decided to hit the road, a cargo pilot on the ground in Manteo made the opposite decision. Like us, he had contacted the weather authorities and received reports that the weather was deteriorating at his destination and in the surrounding areas. But he decided to fly despite the dangerous conditions. Instead of sticking to the approach plate, he used his radar to "paint" the power lines that stretched out over the water and ran on an extended line to the runway he was aiming for. By using these power lines instead of the vertical and horizontal pathway of the approach plate, he thought he could fly a few hundred feet over the water and, with a slight turn, make his way to the runway threshold. He had done it before and it had worked.

Unfortunately, this time the wheels of his aircraft got caught in high-voltage lines, which wrapped themselves around the fuselage, dragging the plane and its occupants into the electrically charged water. Neither the pilot nor the jump-seat pilot made it. The incident took out electricity in a large swath of the northeastern region of the state, where we had been on the road.

Thank goodness I heeded the words of my director of operations that night and didn't break or bend the rules. The drive was long and tiring, but I made it home.

In aviation, as in leadership, when you start taking shortcuts that are just shy of integrity, when you jeopardize the safety of a flight or a project and take actions that are out of line with the truth and what is right, you weaken your position and open cracks that can jeopardize the future stability of your leadership or endeavor.

What would our efforts yield if we required of ourselves and others that we act only with integrity? What if we had the courage to call each other out when we observed breaches? What would our world look like if we were willing to risk our careers to stand up for the truth? As long as manipulative behavior, dishonesty, lies, and immoral acts don't directly affect us, we are too willing to let them go unchallenged. In those defining moments, when we allow a lack of integrity to prevail, we weaken the fabric of our own character.

You know what is right. Listen to that inner voice. Stick to your guns and do the right thing, always.

INTEGRITY

This exercise gives you an opportunity to gain insight into any area of your leadership where your actions are inconsistent with your core beliefs. With recognition comes an opportunity to step back, rethink, and make corrections and choices that are in line with what you stand for. It can be tough to take an honest look at yourself. It's not the easy way, but it is the only way to great leadership.

I. Are You Doing the Right Thing?

1. Do you meet your deadlines? YES ___ NO ___

2. Are you on time? YES ___ NO ___

3. Do you return phone calls and e-mails promptly or have a system to make sure they are returned? YES ___ NO ___

4. Do you deal honestly and forthrightly with employee performance issues? YES ___ NO ___

5. Do you tell higher-ups what they need to hear, rather than what they want to hear? YES ___ NO ___

6. Do you effectively and openly communicate bad news with the knowledge that there is as much to learn from failures, mistakes, and problems as from success? YES ___ NO ___

7. Are you willing to stick to your values and do the right thing, even in the face of losing your own job or hurting your career? YES ___ NO ___

8. Is your compensation plan in line with your company's profitability? YES ___ NO ___

9. Is your compensation plan fair and balanced between levels of employees and executives? YES ___ NO ___

10. Are you regarded as fair and honest? YES ___ NO ___

11. Do you listen to, acknowledge, and value the ideas of others? YES ___ NO ___

12. Do you tell the truth, even in the face of uncertain consequences? YES ___ NO ___

If you answered no to any of these questions, it's time to examine your behaviors and bring them into line with integrity.

II. Keeping Your Word
Have you made decisions or taken actions that are contrary to what you think is right, decisions that are in conflict with your values?

Describe a decision or action that you have taken recently that is inconsistent with what you know to be right:

_____

_____

_____

Address this and bring it back in line with what you believe is the right thing. Write it on your to-do list. Put a date beside it for when you will address and take action on it. Make this commitment visible—a reminder you can't easily avoid. Say you are sorry, rectify any wrongs that might have arisen from conduct that was out of integrity, learn your lesson, and put it behind you.

III. Telling the Truth
Write down something you are not being truthful about, or significant information you are withholding. (No one is looking—this is for you to take a look at you.)

_____

_____

_____

Why you are withholding, hiding, or misstating this truth?

_____

_____

_____

What are possible consequences of telling/sharing the truth?

_____

_____

_____

What are possible consequences of *not* telling the truth, including your emotional and physical well-being, effects on key relationships, and repercussions at work?

_____

_____

_____

Pick a date in the near future and commit to taking action to bring the situation back into line with integrity.

Date: _____

Having integrity is often easier said than done. Being true to your core beliefs, doing the right thing, and standing up for the truth, especially under pressure to waver, is a true test of your leadership character.

2

BALANCE

*Ridiculous yachts, private planes, and big limousines don't make people
enjoy life more . . . they send out terrible messages to the people that work
for you. It would be much better if that money was spent in Africa . . .
it's about getting a balance.*

—RICHARD BRANSON (b. 1950),
CEO of Virgin Group

Iwas a scrawny six-year-old when I learned the lesson of balance the
hard way. My nursery school had a big, hard-packed dirt playground
with two killer seesaws, the old kind built from a solid plank of hardwood anchored in the center with a metal stand. One of my girlfriends
and I raced outside at recess to be the first to claim one of the two. At first
it was fun, but the fun stopped when my friend decided to get off without warning. Unfortunately, I was way up in the air when she hopped off.
My descent was rapid, and the impact sudden and jolting. I wasn't seri-
ously hurt; there was more damage to my psyche than my body. But that
helpless, uncontrolled descent taught me a lasting lesson: when things
start to get wobbly and begin to fall apart, watch out, be vigilant, and do
something before it's too late.

The seesaw is a simple yet important lesson because finding and maintaining balance is an integral part of business, and life. Whether it is our

planet, a person, a product, or an organization, balance is fundamental to sustainability.

The rigors of maintaining business equilibrium begin with you. If you are off-center and unstable, chances are good that your organization will reflect your instability. An interesting thing about balance is that you generally have an innate sense of when you are out of balance. Are you listening to your inner wisdom?

Maintaining balance for leaders extends beyond the self. You also have the extra responsibility of maintaining a balanced organization and workforce. Leaders have many tools to help them gauge and maintain the stability of their endeavors, like reports, trends, ratios, surveys, turnover, and sales. Just as you have an innate sense of being out of balance yourself, as a leader, you should have an inner sense of imbalances occurring in your organization, a sense that something is not right.

Balance is something we feel in our gut.

To understand the role of balance in leadership, let's start with you and take a look at the three main areas of your well-being: mental, physical, and emotional.

MENTAL OVERLOAD

I used to have a lot of stress-related headaches, so I carried a bottle of Tylenol around with me. Those were the start-up days of my early entrepreneurial endeavors, the days when I worked from dawn to dusk with maybe a half day off every week. I pushed myself in every way, and most notably in the mental arena. I didn't have the maturity or wisdom to know when to say enough is enough, when to stop answering the phone, when to say no to one more request. I fell prey to a pattern of mental burnout, which was brought to my attention by resentful employees when I got angry too quickly or cut off discussions that required me to consider alternate points of view. I had not learned the important lesson of regularly stepping away from the weight of the responsibility that comes with being a leader. In retrospect, I realize that I lost some good customers and employees because of my inability to recognize burnout and mental overload and to do something about it before it turned into dysfunction. I know better today. I recognize when the pendulum of mental acuity has swung too far toward exhaustion, and when that happens, I slow down and take a break to bring it back to center. Do you?

At some time in our careers, we go through periods where we are operating at the limits of our mental and intellectual capabilities. Bombarded by too much information, with not enough time off, a jammed schedule of overlapping meetings, and too many deadlines, we begin to lose our perspective. Under relentless pressure from these competing demands, we work harder and longer, thinking we can put off the need to relax and rejuvenate. Our life starts to swing out of control as we lose sight of how to balance the incessant demands of being a leader with the need to give our brains a break.

Leaders need to set an example for others about taking time away from e-mail, instant messaging, texting, phone calls, and the Internet. As a leader, you need to balance your personal life and work commitments and allow others to do the same. Mental overload and stress can show up as impatience, a lack of empathy, and a tendency toward an authoritarian decision-making style. Under the weight of mental fatigue, leaders can lose sight of the big picture and adopt an increasingly short attention span. Do you recognize when you become preoccupied with details and micromanage?

When you are burned out, the effects trickle down into the ranks of the entire organization. With a pressure-cooker at the top, subordinates also become impatient and push those below them, with relentless demands to produce. Collaboration gets waylaid, and control takes over. The meaning behind metrics is ignored as the pendulum continues to swing out of balance, with undue weight resting on the side of results, deadlines, and unsustainable stress. Eventually, employees who can no longer endure the imbalance leave. These are often the best employees, those with a healthy view of the importance a work/life balance. Other less-balanced employees will do what is necessary to conform but will eventually reach the end of their tether and start to exhibit impatience, a lack of empathy, and a methodical, unquestioning, rote addiction to numbers and deadlines.

I have worked with CEOs who are brilliant at financial strategy, with a strong commitment to results and a firm grasp on financial outcomes, operating statistics, and reports. But in striving for financial achievements, they forget to keep a healthy equilibrium between profits and people. Over time, under leadership like this, employee morale begins to erode and turnover increases. I have seen leaders lose their positions in spite of excellent financials because this narrow preoccupation created an instability that threatened the existence of the organization.

These are not the only dangers an organization faces when its leaders mentally burn out. For individuals, operating on the edge can result in damaging consequences: emotional instability, physical breakdowns and health problems, inattention, and inability to focus. Unfortunate consequences can result from extreme behaviors, when people push themselves to the limit. Some people go over the edge and never come back.

I once worked in a factory where a new manager was invited to participate in high-level labor negotiations. He was well liked and respected by his subordinates, good at his job, and happily married with kids. But as the responsibility and his stature increased, he was overly dazzled by the new recognition. He was introduced to fancy restaurants, a lot of alcohol, and fast women—three unfortunate sports of the rough-and-tumble world of behind-the-scenes labor negotiating in this particular industry. Seduced by the high life and the high rollers, he partook of everything liberally. And when his new behavior was found out by his friends, co-workers and family, his marriage fell apart, his friends turned away from him, and he lost the hard-earned respect of his employees.

The importance of maintaining a good mental attitude and recognizing when you are overloaded is really important. The checklist at the end of this chapter will give you an opportunity to assess your attitude toward balance, but my guess is that since you are reading this, you already know where you need to improve.

LEADERS AS PROFESSIONAL ATHLETES

Being a leader often requires that we keep going when others quit. We are the ones who must carry the weight of the challenges and failures of our organization. Like a top athlete, top leadership requires the support of a strong body and constitution. We need to keep our hearts strong, and I mean that literally. Take time out for your body as a regular part of your week: go to the gym, do a workout, take a walk, get a massage. At the very least, leave the confines of your office from time to time, and go outside for a breath of fresh air.

It's important to give your body the right fuel, to eat right and not too much, to drink a lot of water and moderate your intake of alcohol and caffeine. Our bodies are amazing things; when it's time to slow down, take a breather, and rest, they often let us know. They are great barometers for telling us when we are pushing the limits. Unfortunately, we too often ignore the warning signals. Insomnia is taken care of with sleeping aids. We get medication for high blood pressure. We go to fancy restaurants to feel good, and we drink too much, eat too much, smoke, and top it off with a thousand-calorie piece of cake and a cup of coffee. Then we go home and wonder why we can't sleep, and take a pill.

My father was a family doctor who cared about his patients and made house calls regularly. He insisted that we go to our family doctor every year for a checkup. This annual appointment gave our doctor a chance to get to know us, to understand what was normal, and to be sensitive to imbalances in our bodies. For most of us, gone are the days of regular visits to the family doctor; we go to the doctor only in emergencies. Yet we take our cars in every year for an annual maintenance checkup. Why don't we spend that same amount of time checking on the condition of the only chassis we have for our time on earth?

I have worked with more organizations with overweight, stressed-out, hungover executives than I want to count. When I worked at Philip Morris in the early '80s, the Monday-morning budget meeting would be in a fog of smoke, not to mention the bottomless cups of coffee we all drank. Fueled by nicotine and caffeine, there was always a tremendous amount of energy and participation, but we paid for it later in the day, when we became irritable, impatient, and lost focus. In the longer term, many suffered with a lot of sore throats and colds and, sadly, some early encounters with cancer.

When we don't pay attention to our physical health, we stop noticing how bad we feel. We forget what it's like to be vital and alert. Blah is the new normal. When you feel your best, you can do your best. Leaders have a responsibility to be strong for their organizations and their people. You need to be in shape so you can lead others to the finish line. Your body can't take abuse forever. You only have one, and it's got to get you through your whole life. Your physical health is not optional; it is a responsibility that cannot be put off.

OVER THE EMOTIONAL EDGE

We've all had friends, family members, or colleagues who have slipped into emotionally extreme behavior: anxiety, worry, fear, insecurity, anger, or depression. Leaders are hardly immune to emotional imbalances. Human beings have complicated and unique emotional makeups. The difference is that leaders have directly and voluntarily accepted a responsibility toward others. In fulfilling that responsibility, a leader's emotional well-being is a critical stabilizer.

Very often, my executive coaching sessions uncover emotional issues that underlie performance problems. I once coached a manager who was under the gun for not being an effective leader on many counts, ranging from employee morale to customer dissatisfaction. He was ineffective at delegating and inept at handling confrontations. As our sessions evolved, he revealed that he had been severely abused as a child. Those scars were still with him and showed up as a tendency to personalize failures, take offense, and be defensive in the face of constructive feedback. He couldn't get beyond his own insecurities well enough to take the highs and lows of leadership in stride and seek balanced solutions and compromise. Eventually he lost his job as his boss grew weary of having to handle him with kid gloves.

Leaders are not above emotion, as much as we sometimes like to think we are. What distinguishes effective leaders is their willingness and ability to recognize, address, and seek to rise above their weaknesses. We need to be accountable for emotional reactions and emotional outbursts, which can have an adverse effect on others. Theoretically, everyone in life should be responsible for their own bad behaviors—anger, jealousy, greed, selfishness, righteousness, negativity, hatred, resignation, cynicism, depression, addiction, and control. We all have a range of emotional reactions that impede our ability to sustain or engage in positive relationships—anger that alienates us, selfishness that limits our ability to be generous, addictions that hide us from the truth of our deepest insecurities.

It is incumbent on you to seek solutions to your own emotional weaknesses through counseling and personal growth. It is incumbent on you to better yourself and to address those attributes and actions that hold you back.

Great leaders must be the glue that holds their organization together. In the midst of chaos, they must stand firm and stay balanced, they must think clearly and resist the urge to react emotionally when everyone around them is losing control. Emotionally mature leaders must look at both sides of a controversy and know better than to take differences and attacks personally. Emotionally strong leaders must remove themselves from a situation enough to avoid a self-centered reaction to the emotional antics and opinions of others.

Unfortunately, many leaders are out of balance. Heads of state have complicated personal lives, lead corrupt regimes, and enjoy lifestyles characterized by excess or extreme. Business leaders have disproportionate preoccupations with money and metrics. Leaders of important social causes and nonprofits have extreme emotional enmeshment and clouded judgment in the causes they promote. Politicians have unyielding views, believing compromise is giving in.

Tune in to the condition of your emotional well-being. Keep a check on the health of your important relationships. Pay attention to the red flags of anger, lying, and depression. Don't let emotional imbalances persist, and don't allow your pride to get in the way of seeking help when you need it.

Our job is to be exceptional, not just intellectually and physically, but emotionally as well.

As leaders, we are responsible for our own behavior. I once had an instructor in philosophy who told the class that his approach to leading a meaningful life was to identify when and where his behavior adversely affected others, and then take responsibility for changing the suspect behavior. For me, this simple yet powerful message was like a lightning bolt, a vivid indication of how to look at the times in my own life when I danced on the mental, physical, or emotional edge. It caused me to think about the people whom I had pushed to the limit, the times when I fell off cliffs, and all the early warnings that I'd ignored. As I continue to live and learn, I have become much more aware of my own limits and extremes. I try to always be accountable for bringing myself into balance.

As a leader, your mental, physical, and emotional stability is not an option; it is a duty.

A BALANCED ORGANIZATION

As if it's not hard enough to keep yourself balanced, leaders are responsible for keeping their organizations steady and stable as well. It is a constant juggling act: fluctuations in the marketplace, personnel and personality issues, risks versus rewards, deficits and surpluses, fickle customer demands and shareholder expectations, employee satisfaction—all in addition to keeping ourselves straight.

Organizations can be very volatile. Things can be running along smoothly, and then *bam*, a key customer defects. Even more challenging are the slow-moving forces that almost imperceptibly push until a situation is precariously teetering on the edge. It could be a smoldering personnel issue that is not being addressed, or perhaps a cost-saving shortcut that is eroding quality. BP failed to balance a curtailment of expense with the critical importance of ensuring safety through quality. These are the types of threats to stability that leaders must be ever vigilant about. This work isn't for the lighthearted! But it's your job to keep people and projects in equilibrium, listening to and taking into account divergent points of view, and leading teams to compromise for the good of the whole. Fortunately, there are many tools for leaders to use in maintaining a stable and balanced organization.

One of the most basic balancing systems is an organizational chart. When you lay out the functions of your organization on a piece of paper and spell out the relationship between them, to each other, and to the whole, you are providing a balanced platform for your primary functions. Production, Marketing, Finance, Human Resources, IT, and Quality . . . balancing all the different departments will keep your organization strong and stable. If one goes rogue, the whole suffers.

Leaders also have many benchmarks to help them gauge where things are outside of normal operating margins. Executives and analysts rely heavily on financial statements and ratios. There are acceptable limits for different industry groups and acceptable limits in general for debt and equity, profits and losses, and assets and liabilities. There are compensation benchmarks and average costs of employee and executive benefit packages. But organizational charts, metrics, ratios, and reports don't tell the whole story.

Just as important to the health of an organization is the well-being and equilibrium of its workforce. Numbers-driven leaders risk overlooking discontentment and apathy and other human factors that can cause considerable and lasting damage to an organization. When leaders notice signs of dissatisfaction or indications of declining morale, it's time to investigate the root causes, to spend time with managers and staff. Human imbalances, if allowed to grow without correction, can have serious consequences: declining productivity, key employee defection, stress-related absenteeism, and more.

I once consulted for a company that had always attracted the best and the brightest, but a change in leadership precipitated an exodus of executives in response to the difficult new CEO. The board should have been alerted to the possibility of something amiss, but they rationalized and lost an opportunity to make small corrections in a timely manner. Over the next few years, as the defection of talented staff continued, community perception of the company began to decline. When frustration reached a breaking point, key department heads who were the backbone of the institution raised a unified voice against the leadership. By that time, the pendulum had swung pretty far toward the real risk of organizational failure on many fronts. What took only a few years to break would take many more years to rebuild. Finally, after significant damage had been wrought, the CEO was let go and the slow rebuilding and rebalancing process began.

AVERT DANGER BEFORE IT'S TOO LATE

Imbalance is untenable in the long run; eventually something will happen to force a correction. If instability is not alleviated, then collapse is imminent. Destruction is often nature's way of once again creating a level playing field . . . not always the best way to go especially when it concerns people and organizations.

In 2008, Citigroup reported a net loss of $27.7 billion. In that same year, they paid $38.4 billion in compensation and benefits, while Citigroup's stock price fell from a high of $57 in December 2007 to a low of $0.97 in January 2009. To date, Citigroup still owes U.S. taxpayers billions of dollars in TARP (Troubled Asset Relief Plan) funds, and its stock remains in the $4 range. The company had three CEOs between 2003 and 2007.

Losses for Merrill Lynch totaled $35.8 billion in 2007 and 2008. From 1997 to 2008, despite the losses, the board at Merrill Lynch paid over $240 million to three successive CEOs.

In 2007 and 2008, Countrywide Mortgage reported $3.9 billion in losses. Their CEO, Angelo Mozilo, received $250.5 million in performance pay between 2000 and 2008.

Our future will be more secure when leaders balance the science of profitability with the art of people, when they balance short-term demands with an overarching commitment to sustainability. Employees thrive under leaders who are balanced, who understand and practice moderation, and who balance financial contribution with meaningful contribution.

Balance for leaders is an internal and an external responsibility. The fine art of balancing starts with you. Truly great leaders are characterized by stability born of awareness, and they practice balance in all aspects of their lives. Leaders are the fulcrums for their organizations. You are at the center. You are the watchdog for dangerous extremes. Once on the edge, it only takes a small amount of turbulence to bring the whole thing down.

■

PUSHING THE ENVELOPE

In an airplane, the key indicator of balance is the location of the center of gravity (CG). This pivotal point moves forward and backward as a plane is loaded with luggage, passengers, and fuel. For every commercial flight, a mandatory preflight weight and balance calculation is made and verified prior to takeoff, to ensure that the position of the CG is within the acceptable limits according to the aircraft specifications. As a plane approaches the extremes of its limits, it becomes increasingly unstable. On the edge, small disturbances like turbulence or abrupt maneuvers can be fatal.

My first twin-engine plane was a Cessna 310, the same one that Sky King and Penny flew. It was red and white and handled like a sports car. For its size, it had a lot of power, and like a good sports car, the overall handling took some finesse. Like all aircraft, it came with instructions in the form of the pilot's operating handbook. One of the major sections in that handbook is weight and balance. There are sample weight and balance problems, graphs for loading, and the critically important "envelope," the boundaries for the location of the CG. Too far aft and you have a tail-heavy, nose-high aircraft, which presents control problems in a pilot's attempt to keep the nose-high attitude from disturbing the lift needed to keep the airplane flying. If the plane is nose-heavy, landing becomes a challenge as the pilot struggles to keep the nose up when approaching touchdown. Putting too much weight (passengers, luggage) in the rear of a plane results in a tail-heavy, nose-high aircraft. Both extremes introduce control problems for the pilot and can jeopardize the safety of a flight.

On one of my first flights in the 310, I got all of the luggage loaded, but when the first passenger got in, the tail of the plane hit the ground. We rechecked the numbers and consulted the other pilots, but we couldn't see anything wrong with the weight and balance calculations.

Takeoff was fine, but as I leveled off, the controls were what pilots sometimes refer to as "mushy." The plane was definitely favoring a nose-high attitude and the controls were soft; it was uncomfortable for everyone on board. I made some adjustments: I told my passengers in the rear to move forward along with the luggage with the heaviest in the front. That shifted the CG forward. As the flight progressed and we burned off fuel, the CG came even farther forward.

We landed safely in Charleston and bid our somewhat shaken but grateful passengers goodbye. What had gone wrong? We looked once more at the numbers, and to our horror, we discovered that I had used the wrong loading chart. Turning the page, we discovered the chart I was meant to have used. On recalculation, we learned that our CG had been just out of acceptable limits. Shifting the weight forward midflight may have saved our lives.

We should have listened to our gut, which told us that we were not balanced, instead of trusting the metrics. Pilots have to be vigilant in their attention to the effects of weight distribution on the balance and stability of their aircraft. Corrections must be made when the balance is too far aft or too far forward, because exceeding the boundaries can result in fatal consequences. In the same way, leaders must be vigilant in detecting imbalances. When you are in command, everyone looks to you to keep them level and to minimize extremes. You owe it to your followers to be a level-headed, well-adjusted, steady leader.

We all have close calls. We all unintentionally get a little out of balance from time to time. It isn't being imbalanced that is the problem; it's not recognizing it and not taking steps back to center. Balance is a desired state, but it is not static or permanent. The more we are in balance, in every area of our lives, the more sensitive we will be to disruptions. You owe it to yourself and your organization to listen to your instincts, and to be diligent in striving for equilibrium. As the proverb says, "The key to keeping your balance is knowing when you've lost it."

BALANCE

These exercises are designed to help you gain insight into where your life and leadership are out of balance. With that knowledge you can take steps to regain stability, find firmer ground, and seek equilibrium.

I. **Find Your Position on the Seesaw**
   For this exercise, consider three main areas of your life: physical, mental, and emotional.

   Circle the description that best represents the way you feel most of the time. There is space for comments below each.

   Physically, I feel:

   Balanced   Out of balance   On the edge

   Comments:_____

   _____

   Mentally, I feel:

   Balanced   Out of balance   On the edge

   Comments:_____

   _____

   Emotionally, I feel:

   Balanced   Out of balance   On the edge

   Comments:_____

   _____

II. Identify Your Extremes

Below are pairs of opposites. Circle the word in each pair that best describes you.

PHYSICAL

Rested	Tired
Active	Sedentary
Full	Hungry
Moderation	Excess
Clear	Hungover
Low energy	High energy
Healthy	Sick
Well-groomed	Neglected
Underweight	Overweight
Strong	Weak

List considerations regarding your physical well-being:_____

_____

MENTAL

Winning	Losing
Action	Just talk
Decisive	Indecisive
Quiet	Loud
Low risk	High risk
Indifferent	Forceful
Isolated	Collaborative
Acquiescent	Dictatorial

MENTAL (*continued*)

Details	Big picture
Internal	External
Patient	Impatient
Safe	Reckless
Optimistic	Negative

List considerations regarding your mental well-being: _____

_____

EMOTIONAL

Introverted	Extroverted
Truthful	Dishonest
Loving	Hateful
Self-confident	Insecure
Happy	Sad
Generous	Stingy
Grateful	Envious
Intimate	Aloof
Courageous	Fearful
Hopeful	Despairing
Engaged	Disengaged
Suspicious	Trusting
Depressed	Elated

List considerations regarding your emotional well-being: _____

_____

III. Seek Balance

Pick something from each category that you are unhappy about and would like to change. Write them down below. List why you feel that way and what you can do to change. For example, "I feel too busy because I have a huge deadline. I will take a three-day weekend when it is over."

Physically, I feel _____ because _____

_____

_____

To become more balanced, I will: _____

_____

_____

Mentally, I feel _____ because _____

_____

_____

To become more balanced, I will: _____

_____

_____

Emotionally, I feel _____ because _____

_____

_____

To become more balanced, I will: _____

_____

_____

Seeking balance is an ongoing process. What is important is being able to identify extremes and imbalances, and then taking action to bring things back toward equilibrium.

1

AWE

If somebody said before the flight, "Are you going to get carried away look-
ing at the earth from the moon?" I would have said, "No, no way." But
yet when I first looked back at the earth, standing on the moon, I cried.

—ALAN B. SHEPARD, JR. (1932–1998),
Commander, *Apollo 14*

When astronauts get a glimpse of earth from outer space, their appreciation for humanity is elevated through the expanded lens of awe. By most accounts, this unique perspective is life-changing. They see that this round ball that we live on is but a speck in the scheme of the universe. Stephen Hawking reminds us that we are living on one planet, in one solar system, part of one galaxy that is part of a universe filled with at least 100,000 million other galaxies. Scientists have proven that our lifetimes can be measured in fractions of a second when compared to the billions of years preceding human arrival.

Yet despite the preponderance of scientific evidence that reminds us of how small we are, we continue to live our lives with an inflated sense of self-importance and with limited imagination. We heap worry upon worry, we build up stress in response to everyday concerns until it kills us. We get so wrapped up in the details of our lives that we forget how amazing it is to be alive and to be a part of a world filled to the brim with complexity, diversity, and wonder.

Awe pushes us out of this myopic focus and reminds us how amazing it is to be fully alive. This feeling can be inspired by the smallest things: the wide grin of your child in his first school play, the warmth of the sun on your skin after a swim in the ocean. I'm referring to those special times when you look around and realize that in this moment, it doesn't get better than this. It is great to be alive.

Awe can also be evoked in the face of forces of nature, things so powerful and immense that they defy rational understanding, like tornadoes, hurricanes, and earthquakes. These are the times when you look around and think, I hope I live to see another day.

Awe describes those moments when we feel a deep reverence and respect for creation in all of its many forms. Awe helps us to feel alive. It is an attribute that can keep a leader passionately engaged in and appreciative of the business at hand and the people who make it happen. But awe can be elusive for leaders, who, under the weight of great responsibility, can easily lose their sense of wonder and amazement.

As leaders direct and delegate day-to-day activities and manage the intricate interplay of people and projects, they can become distracted by the details. As they move from one tightly scheduled meeting to the next and tackle endless to-do lists, they easily fall prey to the temptations of impatience, rigidity, distraction, control, and a singular focus. Too often they become numb to how amazing it is that so many divergent parts come together to create new products, to invent new ways, and to initiate new services. Fortunate are those leaders who can see with the eyes of an artist or the expansiveness of an astronaut and discern the awesomeness of life and leadership. This ability to appreciate and value life can lift the veil of drudgery and detail to reveal underlying meaning and inspiration.

Awe arouses an appreciation of and a deep respect for our world and all that is within it. It offers a perspective free from self-limiting thought and preoccupation. It opens new doors, allowing you to visualize opportunities that would be inconceivable by the intellect alone. Awe helps redirect focus from yourself to the greater world around you. It adds wonder, amazement, and curiosity to your point of view. Awe holds within it a childlike quality that ironically works to enhance adult maturity.

BUILDING FOR INSPIRATION

One avenue for creating a sense of awe is architecture or office design. What kind of physical environment do you work in? What message do you send to employees and customers when they enter your office? Is it warm and welcoming or dark and cluttered? Is it inspiring and motivational or drab and lifeless?

My cousin is a partner in an investment management firm on Park Avenue in New York. The firm is housed in a soaring glass skyscraper with windows that reflect the color of the sky and capture a sunny or cloudy day on its expansive glass exterior. It is awe-inspiring for me to stand and gaze at the building as it reaches for the sky.

When I had an opportunity to design an office building on the northern beaches of the Outer Banks, I chose to honor the history of the lifesaving stations combined with design features of Thomas Jefferson's Monticello. The result was a welcoming structure with wraparound porches, dormer windows, lazy ceiling fans, and hardwood floors. It was built by local builders and craftsmen, using local materials. The sidewalks were made of "tabby," a historical building material made from oyster shells, water, lime, and ash. And in the middle of the yard was a soothing fountain with a graceful mermaid. The building said, "Welcome! We're glad you're here."

Awe-inspiring workplaces don't have to be expensive. Given the right direction and parameters, even cubicles can capture the imagination and provide an environment for creative ingenuity. Inspirational and meaningful posters on the walls, bulletin boards that display accomplishments, and evidence of customer recognition all foster an environment of appreciation and respect for the work being done. Fresh flowers, lighting, artwork, and employee achievements incorporated into a work environment will help to elevate the staff's perspective above the mundane.

What does your workspace inspire?

TUNE IN TO THE WONDER OF THE WORKFORCE

It's not just bricks and mortar that inspire awe. Human endeavors can also be viewed through the lens of awe, inspiring deep and meaningful appreciation. Innovation, creativity, imagination, and possibility are all sparked by leaders who are able to stand in awe of the potential and power of their employees, products, and services. Workforces, teams, taskforces, departments, divisions—these are all diverse groupings of individuals coming together to create new products, to launch new initiatives, and to seek solutions to stubborn challenges.

I worked at the manufacturing facility of Philip Morris in Richmond, Virginia, after receiving my MBA. My first job was as an internal organizational analyst, and my office was in the basement of a huge factory. It was windowless, had a pungent odor of fresh tobacco leaves, and felt like an underground bunker. Descending into the basement every day and working feverishly in a small cubicle in a shared workspace was very oppressive. To relieve the tedium and alleviate the feeling of being imprisoned in a dungeon, on my breaks I would walk two flights up to the lofty corridors of the executives. Along these hallways were doors leading to viewing platforms that overlooked the factory floor. When I began to lose my perspective, weighed down by the intensity and amount of work, I would head up the stairs to one of these platforms. There I would stand in awe of the bustling efficiency of row upon row of cigarette-making machines spitting out yards of rolled tobacco to be cut up into individual cigarettes at a later point down the line. The floors were spotless, the production lines seamless. Production-line workers seemed to effortlessly come together into a coherent whole for one purpose. It was not dissimilar to what I would imagine a well-ordered beehive might look like. This expansive view of the core operations of Philip Morris gave me the inspiration I needed to go back into my little basement world and do my part.

Complex human endeavors and the systems that support them can inspire awe. Equally impressive are individuals who rise above cultural and social limitations to reach heights of great personal achievement: rags to riches, orphan to congressman, beaten-down worker to respected leader. Space exploration, hadron colliders and particle accelerators, humanitarian efforts, and medical breakthroughs are all worthy of awe and respect. Our world and its people offer an endless spectacle of awe-inspiring accomplishments.

AWE AND INGENUITY

TOMS Shoes is a recent start-up that was inspired by an appreciation and awareness of the needs of others. On a vacation to Argentina, founder Blake Mycoskie's attention was drawn to the many shoeless children exposed to disease and filth. He returned home and created the concept of "one for one": for every pair of shoes he sold, he would donate a free pair to a child without. Today, TOMS is flourishing, with a growing loyal customer base. Their increased contribution to the bottom line is matched with an increase in contribution to needy children in impoverished areas of the world. In 2009, TOMS targeted their donations at 300,000 pairs of shoes.

Shai Agassi, CEO of Better Place, recounted the story of a pivotal and awe-inspiring moment in his life in an interview with *Inc.* magazine. In the shadows of the magnificence of the Arc de Triomphe and the Champs-Élysées in Paris, he pondered two questions. One was, "Do I want to be co-CEO of SAP, one of the largest companies in the world?" The other, a question that had been posed to him at a gathering of Young Global Leaders (a part of the World Economic Forum) was, "How am I going to make a difference in the world?" His decision focused on the latter. He chose to build a company called A Better Place, committed to independence from oil and the development of infrastructure to support the widespread use of electric cars. By his admission, this step outside of the realm of intellectual analysis helped him choose a path that today is making a significant global contribution to weaning us from fossil fuel dependence.

WHAT EVOKES AWE FOR YOU?

What makes you feel that is it great to be alive? It might be a walk down a crowded city street or spending some time with loved ones. It could be a hike through a canyon, a night swim in an ocean lit by phosphorous, a spectacular sunset, or a mountain trail thickly carpeted by pine needles. All of these and more are out there, ready to reawaken your sensitivity to life.

In my work as a consultant, I have witnessed too many office-bound, stressed, clock-driven executives buried under stacks of demands. Their faces are lined with tension, worry, and anxiety. They have forgotten how wonderful and freeing it feels to rise above the details and reconnect with an appreciation of the workplace. I have worked with too many executives whose complexions are pasty, who are overweight, who have bags under their eyes, who sigh constantly. They can barely see relief beyond the deadline of the monthly report on their desk, much less find an appreciation for the big picture of their department and its potential to contribute to the organization. Potential and possibility are obscured by their limited focus on their own feelings of being overwhelmed and their sense of resignation and despair.

CAN WE HAVE A LITTLE FUN?

We all have boarded aircraft where attendants avoid eye contact, where the air is oppressive, and where the overall atmosphere borders on hostile. We endure flights where pilots introduce themselves over the PA system to passengers as if they were reading a script, welcoming you aboard with all the enthusiasm of a wet mop.

I had such an experience on a cross-country flight recently. Try as I may, I was unable to establish eye contact with the flight attendant. And it wasn't personal; from my vantage point he didn't connect with anyone on board. His indifference to the passengers pervaded the in-flight service and the safety announcements. I hoped that this wouldn't be a flight where I would actually need his assistance, because when it came down to life, it didn't seem like he cared much about mine or his.

On another recent flight on a commuter airline, I had the opposite experience: a pilot who stepped out of the cockpit and welcomed me aboard and flight attendants who smiled, looked me in the eye, and anticipated my needs. The crew laughed and exuded a lightheartedness that made the flight an enjoyable experience.

Quite different experiences for similar circumstances. The first, distant and devoid of vitality; the second, vibrant and full of life. This is not unique to the airlines. These distinctions can be seen in almost every type of business or service.

Leaders create these distinctions through their expectations and the culture that they command. What kind of environment do you provide for your staff? What impression do others have on entering your organization or company? What does your reception area say about your leadership? What kind of atmosphere does your organization foster? What kind of message do your employees send out to customers? Is your company imbued with a sense of appreciation and respect?

APPRECIATION SUPPRESSORS

Three seductive and compelling temptations that often cloud a leader's ability to connect with awe are time, an inflated sense of self-importance, and a narrow focus on results.

Time begins its work of suppressing inspiration and awe when you start your day by barely acknowledging your children or your spouse as you rush to make it to work, catch a flight, or get to a meeting. Inspiration and awe are buried deeper as you hurry past the security guard, the receptionist, and the administrative team without a kind greeting. Once in your office, you are bombarded with phone calls, e-mails, appointments, demands, and requests. Before you know it, you are living in a world of not enough time. You tell yourself that you will attend to your health, your spouse, the gym, your friends, your children, even yourself—later. But so often, there is no later. Your life as a leader has become routinely way too busy. The grandeur of what you and your staff accomplish and contribute to rarely has time to sink in. Awe is buried under piles of reports and graphs. What is it all for, if not to make your life and the lives of others more fulfilling, more challenging, and more awesome?

Self-importance is an easy trap to fall into when you are at the top. The president, the commander, the CEO—you are the one everybody looks up to, the one everybody turns to when they are at the end of the line, the one who has the solutions and can save the day and the organization. Leaders are constantly looked up to, especially great leaders. If you are financially successful, there are people who kowtow to you and put you on a pedestal. When you sit in the big office and are constantly called on to be the final referee, it's easy to feel self-important. Just the nature of being at the helm puts you in a position where many people think that you are special. Self-focus becomes very tempting when it seems to soothe the often bruised and battered egos of leaders in today's often antagonistic business climate.

But humility opens many doors, and the ability to experience awe and have a keen appreciation for the world around you are two of them. It's important to keep a vigilant watch over the threat of self-aggrandizement and egocentric thinking. A cold and distant leader can have a chilling effect on others.

You *are* important, but so is everyone else. When you begin to see the world within the context of yourself only, your ability to discern amazement recedes into a foggy distance. When you lose your ability to feel and experience awe in the face of humanity and all of its complexity, it is time to step away from the fray and seek a fresh perspective.

A NARROW FOCUS

Preoccupation with numbers and details is another enemy of awe. Be cautious about being overly focused on the numbers side of leadership. The value of money and profits rests in how they can improve life. Numbers in and of themselves are meaningless. If you make a ton of money and have no time to enjoy it, share it, or use it in ways that benefit others, then what's the point? If you die rich but unhappy and alone, you missed the boat.

Awe is an eye-opener. Take a good look at the people around you. Consider the multitude of talents and skills that are focused and directed to the work required by your leadership. Take a moment to watch a clerk doing data entry; try it yourself. Walk late-night halls filled with silence. Be aware of the technologies that support your business. Look behind the financial reports to see the depth of activities that make the numbers real. Stand on the trading floor or sit behind a bond trader for a morning. Seek out and listen to the stories of the people whose lives you affect. Get out from behind your desk. Step away from the office. Take a moment or two to appreciate your position and your opportunity to positively influence the lives of others. Open your doors and windows, breathe, take it in . . . live!

IPOs IN THE MOONLIGHT

The view from the cockpit of a small propeller airplane is a lot different from that of a rapidly climbing, high-altitude-seeking jet. In a four-seat Cessna without pressurization and oxygen, you are limited to flying at or below about 10,000 feet, or just under two miles above the surface. At those lower altitudes, you get a bird's-eye view of the world below while retaining a sense of reality and perspective lost at 30,000 feet. Flying at 1,000 feet is even more interesting: you're high enough to get the big picture, but low enough to see sharks trolling near the breakers and people cutting grass in their yards. At South-East Air we offered those "above it all but still connected" flights.

Many of our most valued passengers were high-level leaders and corporate executives vacationing on the Outer Banks with their families. Often they had to return to big cities along the Northeast Corridor for important meetings or presentations. They called SouthEast Air to get them there and back in as short a time as possible. When customers called our reservation line, they were always greeted with courtesy and professionalism. Because of this and the major-airline-sounding name of the company, first-time passengers generally expected our small airline to have jets, flight attendants, air-conditioned aircraft, and high altitudes. However, in the early days of the business, what arrived to pick them up was a four-seater, single-engine, high-winged plane with a youngish pilot in khaki shorts. Depending on the season, customers might also be greeted with a very sweaty handshake, as summer days were often sweltering. The best hope of air-conditioning in small planes are cooler temperatures at higher altitudes.

Often our waiting passengers were dressed for business: carefully tailored suits, pressed shirts, and elegant ties. When they realized that the small plane approaching the tarmac was for them, initial reactions ranged from mild anger and fear to shocked amusement. However, as courageous leaders do, they bravely stepped into the copilot seat, put on a headset, strapped themselves in, and prepared for an adventure.

One afternoon in the summer of 1997, I landed at First Flight Airport, a small 3,000-foot strip next to the Wright Brothers Memorial, to pick up one of those well-dressed businessmen. We were heading to Teterboro Airport just outside of New York City, where he was attending a celebratory dinner at the Four Seasons restaurant to mark the successful IPO of a deal he had underwritten.

On the trip up, I assuaged his unease by explaining the instruments and their functions. We talked about our respective career paths. We casually observed and remarked on the procession of cities passing below us. After a two-hour flight, we landed in Teterboro, where he was whisked away by a waiting limousine. I headed to the pilot's lounge to wait for his 11:00 p.m. return and our flight back to the beach.

He showed up just after 11:00, a little inebriated and in great spirits. He said that one of the highlights of the evening had been his tale of the flight up in a little plane, much to the amazement of the well-heeled jet-setters in attendance. He told me that his vivid descriptions of the four-seater plane, the casually dressed CEO doing double-duty as a pilot, and the experience of being in the cockpit and listening in to the chatter of the airline world kept everyone at the party entertained.

After a quick call to flight service, we walked out onto the tarmac, got into the plane, radioed the tower, got our clearance, buckled up, and started the engine. We were the only airplane heading out to the runway. The largely deserted late-night airfield was a spectacle of blue and white taxiway lights, punctuated by the green/white/green/white flash of the rotating beacon. As we took off, air traffic control turned us toward Manhattan at 2,000 feet, keeping us out of the flight paths of any commercial airliners in the area.

It was a beautiful, clear night. The sky above and the earth below were carpeted with twinkling lights and stars. The moon was full. As we flew toward Manhattan and turned south, we could distinguish Central Park as a big shadow in the middle of headlights making yellow contrails on the city streets. As we left the city and began our voyage over the harbor and toward the Atlantic Ocean, Lady Liberty extended her hand to us. To our left lay the vast, unforgiving dark Atlantic Ocean, to the right the bright skyline of Philadelphia, and behind us the receding light display of New York. This was our mesmerizing view as we headed toward the less-populated coastal towns of New Jersey and Delaware.

I looked over at my passenger. He sat serenely in his rumpled and sweat-stained shirt, his jacket carelessly thrown on the backseat. Sitting in the copilot seat with a headset on, he listened in to the foreign language of controllers as he gazed out on the panoramas that enveloped us. The night sky, the canopy of stars, the twinkling lights below, and the dull but constant hum of the engine were hypnotic. With our attention held by the amazingly beautiful scene, neither of us said a word as we cut through the night sky and continued south.

When we arrived back at the airport, well after midnight, the investment banker helped tie the plane up, and we went our separate ways, he back to a vacation and I back to work in a few hours. I hope that the combination of the flight and the vacation made room in his crowded mind for new thoughts, perhaps new perspectives. For me, that flight renewed my appreciation for the company I was building and the service it provided. The airline business is tough, but at the center of my commitment to it was a deeper commitment to all of the people who loved the Outer Banks but needed convenient and expedient transportation to get there.

Flying low over Manhattan on a moonlit night, paralleling a massive thunderstorm filled with lightening, watching the sunrise over the Atlantic from a mile up, cruising at 500 feet offshore and spotting pods of dolphins . . . those were the times I would remember why I was doing it, why I was working so hard and investing so much. My trusty Cessna was always ready to elevate me and my view of my world, providing me with inspiration and appreciation for being alive.

So keep a good perspective. Stay infatuated with your life. Restart your battery when you lose the spark of wonder. Appreciate awe and seek it out. Include awe and its expansive viewpoint in your business life. Let it flavor your leadership. Let it inspire and uplift you. Take the time to step back and be humble. Allow the awesomeness of your work and efforts and the contributions of others sink in. Step back and stand in awe.

AWE

I. You and Awe

For a quick and honest assessment of your current receptivity to awe, answer the following questions on a scale of 1 to 4:

1 often
2 sometimes
3 seldom
4 never

1. I take unscheduled walks throughout my organization, observing day-to-day operations and enjoying informal conversations with employees from many departments.

    1   2   3   4

2. I feel moved in the face of incredible beauty (music, art, nature).

    1   2   3   4

3. I am grateful for my life.

    1   2   3   4

4. I find time to enjoy the simple pleasures of life (playing with children, listening to music, taking a walk, appreciating nature).

    1   2   3   4

5. I feel fully alive and vibrant.

    1   2   3   4

6. I acknowledge and recognize those who have contributed to where I am today.

    1   2   3   4

7. I'm glad that I'm a leader.

    1   2   3   4

8. I'm comfortable being alone and quiet, allowing my thoughts and my imagination to wander.

    1   2   3   4

Add up your answers.
Your Score _____

A lower score indicates an appreciation for the expansiveness and wonder of the world and humanity. A higher score means you might be viewing the world with blinders, unable to see the wonder and awe in what is going on in your organization and your life. Perhaps you are burned out, highly stressed, and under too much pressure. Step away from distractions and seek ways to renew your sense of appreciation.

II. **Make a Date With Awe**

Below is a list of things you can do to reconnect with awe. Circle four that you will commit to over the next few months, and put a target date by each.

1. Pick a couple of hours during the workweek to be unplugged: turn off your phone, e-mail, iPad, laptop, and any other device that distracts you. If necessary, let people know, cover your bases. Use the time to walk around work and have casual conversations and reconnect with employees.

2. Volunteer for a local community cause. If you can make the time, travel to a disaster-stricken area as a volunteer.

3. Hike up a mountain, into a canyon, or through a forest.

4. Sit alone in a comfortable place and listen to beautiful music for thirty minutes or more.

5. Watch a sunset or a sunrise.

6. Sit on a park bench and watch people—without judgment, just curiosity.

7. Attend meetings in other departments just out of interest, to see what they're doing.

8. Go to an art museum.

9. Attend a concert or symphony.

10. Take a scenic airplane ride.

11. Sign up with Virgin Galactic for a flight into outer space (www.virgingalactic.com/booking).

12. Observe a nursery school or kindergarten class.

13. List other activities that would elevate your appreciation and curiosity for life: _____

To experience awe you must be able to appreciate your world, to sense its wonder, to feel alive.

> The important thing is not to stop questioning. Curiosity has its own reason for existing. One cannot help but be in awe when he contemplates the mysteries of eternity, of life, of the marvelous structure of reality. It is enough if one tries merely to comprehend a little of this mystery every day. Never lose a holy curiosity.
>
> —ALBERT EINSTEIN

LIFTOFF

What effect can a single individual have in these cataclysmic times? The answer lies in that quality with which man only of all earthly life is gifted. In each man is a spark, able to kindle new fires of human progress, new light for the human spirit. This ember may lie dormant through centuries of darkness or it may be fanned to flames by the winds of a crisis, sweeping over the earth, bringing life to others with its light and warmth. When enough of these fires are burning, they create a new dawn of spiritual understanding; the flame of a great people is formed.

—CHARLES A. LINDBERGH (1902–1974)
(*Of Flight and Life*, Yale University Press: 1947)

The countdown is over, the checklists complete. All systems are go. It is time for liftoff. And you are in command.

The success of your leadership flight, from liftoff to touchdown, will depend on the strength of your foundation. What is yours made of? Are you a leader respected for your steadfast integrity? A leader of great courage with the strength to face conflict? A visionary with a keen eye for opportunity? You alone are responsible for the integrity of your foundation and the distinguishing character of your leadership flight. It is up to you to choose what you stand for and what values you represent. Whatever yours are, they will shape and define your unique leadership gifts, if you recognize and use them.

Remember your core values. Keep them in sight. Refer to them when you need to regain a sense of purpose. Use your values to keep you on course and guide you to your destination. The values you have identified in this book are just as relevant to the effectiveness of your leadership as any strategies and goals, because who you are as a leader is much more than your financial acumen and business savvy. You might be a brilliant strategist, an adept negotiator, a firm task-master, an excellent communicator. You can take classes and read books and stay up to date with the latest management theories. You can have the science of business down pat. But without a foundation of meaning and purpose, work and life lose their value. Without a commitment to improving life, livelihoods, and society, you will be buffeted by external forces and wander in a futile attempt to find meaning in materialism. True purpose resides within you; you need only look inside for the foundation that girds your character and the fuel you need to ignite your strengths and propel the delivery of your unique contributions to the world around you.

Let *LiftOff Leadership* serve as your guide to purpose and meaning. Use the insights *you* have gained herein to seek avenues for continued personal growth and development. Return to these pages and checklists when it's time to reassess, and take a good look at yourself to see where you can improve. Then go forward with a renewed appreciation for the impact you have on the quality of the many lives under your influence: employees, customers, shareholders, and the broader community. Step up to the responsibility of being a leader with humility, and renew your commitment to contributing not just financially but in meaningful and beneficial ways to humanity.

As you close this flight guide and reenter the world of leadership, take a moment to reflect on the culture that surrounds you. Are your employees engaged and productive? Is their morale high? Are your customers satisfied? Is the work environment positive and vibrant? Are people accountable, engaged, and willing to take risks? What you see is a reflection of who you choose to be as a leader. Let your best values be the torchbearers for your conduct. *Never forget* the influence that your leadership has on the people around you. Remember that you have an opportunity to make a positive difference in your organization and in the lives of your employees. Strive to elevate potential and bring purpose and meaning into work.

One day you will walk away from the leadership position you now hold. When you look back, what will you see? Your leadership story will be written on the faces of the people you leave behind. Your legacy will be evidenced in the integrity and sustainability of your products and services. It will be reflected in the loyalty and satisfaction of your customers. Who you were and what you stood for will be imprinted on the lives and livelihoods of those you led.

When all is said and done and the flight is over, be a leader who can look back and say with confidence, "I did my best, and I gave my best. The world is a better place because I was a leader."

ACKNOWLEDGMENTS

There are milestones in our lives, points in time when a novel insight reveals a new possibility, a different direction. One of those milestones for me was on my fifty-fifth birthday, when I realized that the sum total of my life's choices, circumstances, and consequences had occurred for a reason. It was at that moment that I knew it was important to write a book for leaders.

Little did I know at the time what kind of challenge I had taken on. I knew very little about writing a book and less about the publishing field. But like a good entrepreneur, I was fueled by passion and intrigued by the possibilities. I willingly jumped off the "book writing" cliff with faith that I would grow my wings on the way down and eventually soar.

I must admit that writing a book wasn't an easy flight for me. I am indebted to Eric Kampmann of Midpoint Trade and Beaufort Books for having the courage to take on a first-time author. I am ever so grateful to Margot Atwell, Associate Publisher, who had the guts to stand up for nothing less than my best. Thank you, Margot, for pushing me beyond my perceived limitations, and thank you for assembling a great team of professionals who have been committed, accountable, and fun to work with.

In addition, I could not have produced this book and developed its platform without Sara Birkemeier of 8 Dot Graphics, the professionals at Monteiro & Company PR, expert editors and writers Mina Samuels and Marcia Horowitz, Diane Paces-Wiles of Alchemie Consulting, proofreaders Oriana Leckert and Lynne and Bill Reed of Misty Valley Books, media expert Aaron Caswell of AG Productions, Uta Jehnich of Speakers Intel Services, and Julie Dreelin of Beach Productions. I believe in surrounding myself with the best, and you guys are it!

This book could not have been written without my thirty-five years of experience as a leader. To those who were instrumental in the development of my leadership character: Dr. Charles McClung, Malcolm Wilder, William Patterson, Lillie Cox-Branch, Lee Tait, Bob Bryant, Bill Van Arnam, the Brindleys, and the many outstanding leaders who were B&B on the Beach homeowners (notably Fred Bischoff, John Guffey, and Les Schmidt) and shared their wisdom with me over many a glass of wine at The Blue Point . . . thank you. And to the institutions that shaped me further: The University of Virginia, Virginia Commonwealth University, The College of William and Mary, Philip Morris USA, Girl Scouts, and the Federal Aviation Administration—their values, curriculum, and training show up in these pages.

Not only is leadership an art and a science, but true leadership arises from one's heart. I gratefully acknowledge my family whose love gave me the confidence to be a leader: my mother, Betty Shotton, Sr., my father, Dr. Donald Shotton, and my two sisters, Jean Stone and Lynne Reed, who to this very day keep a careful watch over their little sister. To my cousins the Butlers and Bob Wyckoff, exceptional leaders themselves, thanks for your willingness to lend a hand when needed. And to my best friends Rebecca and Carson, who have been there to hold my hand through every storm, helping me to reach the sunshine. I also acknowledge my community, Ocracoke Island. It must be the best place on earth, not just because of its beaches and its beauty, but because of its people. Thanks to all of you who faithfully asked "how's the book coming along?" and tolerated my introversion and preoccupation over the long years of writing.

Special thanks to Barbara Lombardo Reynolds, formerly of Monteiro & Company, whose belief in the importance of the book's message for today's leadership climate and belief in me truly made this all possible. She represents the strength of one person's conviction to make a difference.

And to my best teacher of all, those of you who had the grace to allow me the privilege and honor of being your leader, especially the awesome, never-to-be-repeated teams at B&B on the Beach, Brindley & Brindley, SouthEast Air, and Sea Air. Thank you.

And finally to Chris and Aslan, for encouraging me to be me and in that act, allowing this book to be a true expression of my life's purpose.

Betty Shotton

Ocracoke, North Carolina

September, 2011

ABOUT THE AUTHOR

Betty Shotton is a lifelong leader, CEO, and serial entrepreneur. She is an advocate for meaningful and principled leadership.

Through speaking and writing Betty seeks to broaden leadership perspectives and chart a new course for the future. She reminds leaders that numbers and financial acumen alone are not sufficient indicators of success. True success is obtained when finance and humanity are balanced in a model that contributes in meaningful ways to organizations and society.

During her professional career, Betty has founded and led six companies, including one that was part of an NYSE IPO known today as ResortQuest International, a part of Wyndham Worldwide. In a commitment to establishing air transportation for her community, she started two regional air carriers, SouthEast Air and SeaAir. During her tenure in aviation leadership, she periodically joined the flight teams as a commercial pilot. She is one of approximately 850 women in the US with an ATP rating (Air Transport Pilot).

Betty is a graduate of The University of Virginia, and a member of the first class of women admitted to the once all-male school. She studied at the Graduate Business School of William & Mary and completed her MBA in Marketing & Human Resources at Virginia Commonwealth University.

Betty lives on Ocracoke Island and in Black Mountain, North Carolina, with her husband, Chris Hyland.

LEADERSHIP CHECKLISTS from the book are available for download at:
http://liftoffleadership.com/leader-resources/checklists-self-assessments/

For SPEAKING ENGAGEMENTS please refer to:
http://liftoffleadership.com/presentations/
www.liftoffleadership.com

INDEX

NOTES

NOTES

NOTES

NOTES